Catch'd on Fire

The Journals of Rufus Hawley,
Avon, Connecticut

NORA OAKES HOWARD

THE
History
PRESS

Published by The History Press
Charleston, SC 29403
www.historypress.net

Front cover: Excerpt from Rufus Hawley's journal, January 1807. *Photograph by John Pecora. Hawley-August Collection, Avon Free Public Library*; Landscape, undated, by George Edward Candee (1837–1907), of the Rufus Hawley homestead, 281 Old Farms Road, Avon, CT. The three children are likely Hawley family members; in the distance are the Farmington River and the spire of the Avon Congregational Church. *Photograph by John Pecora. Private collection.*

Back cover: Portrait of Edward Eugene Hawley (1811–1868), grandson of Reverend Rufus Hawley. Edward, the family historian and caretaker of his grandfather's journals, lived in the Hawley house for over thirty years. He is perhaps the closest relative to Reverend Hawley whose likeness survives. *Photograph by John Pecora. Hawley-August Collection, Avon Free Public Library*; Burning of Avon's first meetinghouse in 1817. Painting by Janice Loeffler, circa 1988. *Photograph by Wick Mallory. Collection of the West Avon Congregational Church. Used with permission of the Avon Historical Society.*

First published 2011

ISBN 978-1-5402-2962-5

Library of Congress Cataloging-in-Publication Data

Howard, Nora.
The journals of Rufus Hawley, Avon, Connecticut / Nora Oakes Howard.
p. cm.
Includes bibliographical references (p.   ) and index.
ISBN 978-1-5402-2962-5
1. Hawley, Rufus, 1741-1826. 2. Congregational churches--Connecticut--Avon--Clergy--
Biography. 3. Avon (Conn.)--Biography. I. Title.
BX7260.H312H69 2011
285.8092--dc23
[B]
2011035623

For Roger

and our sons

Jackson Oakes Howard and Samuel Volney Righter Howard

Rufus Hawley devoted his life to a parish that became the town of Avon.

In 1817, his meetinghouse burned clear to the ground.

According to legend, he may have set the fire.

CONTENTS

CONTENTS

ACKNOWLEDGEMENTS

Three books inspired this biography. Laurel Thatcher Ulrich's riveting story of a Maine woman in *A Midwife's Tale: The Life of Martha Ballard Based on Her Diary, 1785–1812* set my course. I found my subject in Mary-Frances MacKie's *Avon* and Christopher Bickford's *Farmington*, both of which contained tantalizing excerpts from Rufus Hawley's journals. Robert and Gladys August of Avon, Connecticut, owned the journals, and I am indebted to them for allowing me access to their collection. In 2002, the Augusts generously donated the Hawley archives to the Avon Free Public Library. To Gladys, and to the late Bob August, I owe my deepest gratitude.

During the ten years that I have been researching Rufus Hawley's life, I have appreciated the assistance of many individuals and organizations. The Avon Free Public Library's executive director, Virginia Vocelli, oversees the Hawley collection and was helpful beyond measure. Assistant director Donna Miller and reference librarian Patrice Celli also provided information and encouragement.

Teri Wilson, president of the Avon Historical Society, assisted me in every way possible. Reverend John Van Epps, archivist of the United Church of Christ–Connecticut Conference, and consultant Emily Holcombe provided expert proofreading. Wick Mallory, of the West Avon Congregational Church, helped me transcribe Rufus Hawley's journals, a process that took seven months and ran to one thousand typed pages. West Avon Congregational Church historian Jeannie Parker and staff member Marj Bender guided me to compelling details and allowed me access to the church's vital records

(1751–1860), which I entered into a database. This biography also benefited from research by Rufus Hawley's descendants: Edward Eugene Hawley, Reginald Birney and Richard Temple.

Dr. Kevin Sweeney's Yale University dissertation, "River Gods and Related Minor Dieties," provided insight into Rufus Hawley's education at Hatfield Academy. Avon cemetery guides, painstakingly compiled by the late Marian E. and Ruth A. Thompson, were invaluable. Sally Cowles and Betty Guinan, historians of East Granby, and Jennifer Vazquez, Cider Brook Cemetery historian, kindly shared their research. Three photographers contributed their work to this book, for which I am very grateful: independent photographers Wick Mallory and Peter Wright, and John Pecora, of Autograph, in Farmington.

I appreciated the expert assistance of librarians and archivists at Yale University, Harvard University, the American Antiquarian Society, the Avon Free Public Library, the Connecticut Historical Society, the Connecticut State Library, the Harriet Beecher Stowe Center, the Farmington Room at the Farmington Library, the Salmon Brook Historical Society and the Simsbury Genealogical and Research Library. Officials in the offices of the town clerks in Avon, Farmington and Simsbury helped with probate and land records. Cliff McCarthy, curator of the Stone House Museum of the Belchertown Historical Association, and his colleague Shirley Bock opened their collection to me and provided background about Rufus Hawley's mentor, Reverend Justus Forward. Paul Kramer transcribed the Civil War correspondence between Edward Hawley and his son Eugene.

For inviting me to speak about Rufus Hawley, I thank the Association for the Study of Connecticut History, the Hawley Society, the Stanley-Whitman House, the United Church of Christ–Connecticut Conference, the Avon Congregational Church, the West Avon Congregational Church, the Avon Inter-faith Brunch and the Turkey Hills Study Club. During my research, I also benefited from the support of good friends who found the story compelling: Gail Alvord, Senia Bachir-Abderahman, Reverend Rosemary Baue, Francie Brown Holmes, Lorrie McElligott, Nina Schmid, Elizabeth Swain, Gigi Burke, Reverend Krysia Burnham, Reverend Kenneth Fuller, Suzy Love and Anthony O'Neill.

Rufus Hawley's pulpit descendants at the West Avon Congregational Church, Reverend Dr. Donald Ketchum and Reverend Dr. Brian Hardee, have patiently awaited this biography. Two other pastors deserve special recognition: Reverend Evans Sealand of the First Congregational Church of Canton Center and archivist (retired) of the United Church of Christ–

Connecticut Conference and Reverend Edward T. Falsey, former pastor of the breakaway Avon Congregational Church. Both enthusiastically provided pieces to the puzzle.

I am especially grateful to The History Press and to my editor, Jeffrey Saraceno, for bringing this story to publication.

INTRODUCTION

The inscription on Rufus Hawley's headstone is barely legible, and four rusty rods hold the stone together. The story of his ordinary life in Avon, Connecticut (then called Northington), from 1768 to 1826 has never been told. As it turns out, he quietly wrote his own story in thirty-three journals four inches wide, composing a few lines daily in diminutive cursive. Although seventeen journals during this fifty-year span are missing, the steady pattern of his record keeping points to the likelihood that at one time these journals existed.

This biography is based on these journals, along with church minutes, vital records and a multitude of other sources. Still, Rufus Hawley remains elusive, and the tools a biographer customarily uses seem lost. I have never read a sermon he delivered, seen a picture of his face or found more than one of his letters. I am confident, however, that he would feel his story received a careful and honest look.

To experience the rhythms he followed, I present the story in sections, many one year in length, often using his own words and irregular spelling. While his routine entries are like clockwork, events of chaos, destruction and risk burst out unexpectedly.

Rufus Hawley's journals (he did not call them diaries) start in 1763, when he was a twenty-one-year-old student at Hatfield Academy in Massachusetts and on his way to Yale College. Ordained in 1769 as pastor of Northington, he wrote of epidemics and smallpox, encounters with the military during the American Revolution, neighborhood tragedies and life with seven children.

He never traveled more than about fifty miles from home, except for three trips (in 1805, 1811 and 1821) to the Western Reserve in Ohio. He wrote his last journal in 1812, when he was seventy-one years old.

Fire is a recurring theme in Rufus Hawley's life—fires of destruction and spiritual fires that smoldered and sometimes ignited. His journals show him as a student, farmer, pastor, nephew, cousin, uncle, son, brother, husband, father and grandfather. His wife, Deborah Kent Hawley, gave birth to six boys: Timothy Ruggles, Rufus Forward, George Washington, Jesse Dudley, Orestes Kent and Zerah. At long last, a daughter arrived—Sophia.

His network of colleagues, friends and relatives was wide; the names of 200 ministers and 1,150 other people appear in the journals. Reverend Hawley baptized Wilford Woodruff, who became the fourth president of the Mormon Church. He was a colleague of Lemuel Haynes, the first African American minister ordained in a Protestant denomination. Rufus Hawley knew antislavery orator Reverend Jonathan Edwards Jr. He loved his year at Yale College and his lifelong association with New Haven.

Always beginning a day's entry with the weather, Rufus recorded the facts, corrected some misspelled words and drew a cross or a tiny hand with a pointed finger to direct attention to important entries. Outliving two wives, one child and almost all his contemporaries, he almost single-handedly built one community of faith. Then it all fell apart.

His grandson Edward Eugene Hawley described Reverend Rufus's son Rufus Forward Hawley as strong and with extraordinary powers of endurance. Rufus Hawley must have had these traits himself, for he often wrote of times when he needed all the strength he could muster. Bearing the parish's troubles, he went anywhere on a moment's notice to bolster faith and offer reassurance. He kept his head and heart when it surely seemed like he just might do otherwise.

This is the story of the early history of Avon, through the private journals of the man who held the most important position in the parish.

1

RUFUS HAWLEY, 1741–1762

O n February 21, 1741, Rufus Hawley was born in Farmington, Connecticut. His parents were Timothy Hawley, a farmer, and Rachel Forward Hawley. Rufus's grandfather, Captain Joseph Hawley of Farmington, served twelve terms in the Connecticut General Assembly; his great-great-grandfather, Thomas Welles, was governor of Connecticut.

Rachel Forward and Timothy Hawley had married in 1736. She had grown up in Simsbury's parish of Turkey Hills (today East Granby) on a farm with cows, sheep, pastures and an apple orchard. Timothy Hawley was a widower, and he had a son, Thomas, age five, and a daughter, Abigail, age two (who died five years later in 1741). Rachel may have brought to the marriage some of the sixty pounds of money her father had given her. After her father's death several years later, she inherited seventy pounds and a large brass kettle.

Rufus grew up with his half brother, Thomas, whom he always called his brother; his older brother, Jesse (born 1738); and with Abigail (born 1743) and Deborah (born 1746). The Hawleys' 116-acre farm, with a barn, a cow house and an orchard, was located between today's Mountain Spring Road and Route 10, in the area of the Farmington Country Club. Timothy's father, Captain Joseph Hawley, lived next door to the east, and shops and craftsmen were a short walk away. Also nearby was the meetinghouse, completed in 1714, fifty feet square and two stories high, with an upstairs gallery for the youth.

Reverend Samuel Whitman most likely baptized baby Rufus at a time when Reverend Jonathan Edwards was leading the Great Awakening's religious revival throughout southern New England. Reverend Whitman, in the final decade of his almost fifty-year pastorate, delivered sermons calmly and with scholarly precision.

In the spring of 1752, when Rufus was eleven years old, the family moved fifteen miles north to Turkey Hills. Timothy Hawley had sold his Farmington farm for 2,600 pounds to Samuel Woodruff, reserving one-third of the orchard's fruit for his father. Traveling to their new home, the Hawleys rode through Farmington's parish of Northington and on to Simsbury. Timothy Hawley had paid 2,000 pounds for an eight-part share in a sawmill, along with a farmhouse, a barn and two hundred acres with a large marsh of almost four acres to the east.

The Turkey Hills parish of Simsbury was divided in half by the Metacomet Ridge, a narrow, mountainous trap rock ridge stretching from New Haven to Vermont. The Hawleys lived on the ridge's west side, which had the Salmon Brook meetinghouse. East side residents had the Turkey Hills meetinghouse and proximity to the town of Suffield. Each side of Turkey Hills had its own schoolhouse. Simsbury's population was about 2,250 people, and seven African Americans, called servants in inventories and wills, lived in the parish of Turkey Hills about the time of the Hawleys' move. Rufus's uncle Abel Forward owned two slaves, and his uncle Joseph Forward owned a slave named Jenny.

The Turkey Hills woods had honey, berries, nuts and mushrooms. There were salad greens such as watercress, cowslip, milkweed, dandelions and ferns. Game was plentiful: deer, bears, squirrels, rabbits, geese, ducks, pigeons and turkeys. The fields and orchards had apples and pears, Indian corn, hay, blue-flowered flax, wheat, rye, oats and potatoes. Gardens were filled with beans, squash, peas, pumpkins, cucumbers, carrots, parsnips and beets. In the barnyards and pathways were cows, sheep, horses, pigs and poultry. The Farmington River and the mighty Connecticut River were nearby, with eels, shad and salmon. Local stores carried necessities and niceties: earthenware, indigo, beads, thread, pins, needles, silk, velvet, lace, paper, books, jackknives, salt, molasses, spices and sugar.

Rufus's neighbor in Turkey Hills was his cousin Justus Forward. Justus emerges in the journals as the most influential person in Rufus's life. Eleven years older than cousin Rufus, Justus had grown up on the east side of the Metacomet Ridge. Inspired by the Great Awakening to become a minister, Justus, at eighteen, was making plans to attend Yale College when tragedy struck his family.

During three weeks in July and August 1748, four of Justus Forward's younger brothers and sisters died from what he called the "sore sickness," possibly scarlet fever: Dan, age twelve; Charity, seven; Rachel, five; and

Samuel, three. For the next two years, his parents could not bear to let Justus leave home. Justus's father, Joseph, said to his son in 1766 on his deathbed, "You know how difficult it was for me when you went to learning." But Joseph had always wanted one of his sons to be a minister, a calling he himself had been unable to attain.

Justus finally entered Yale in 1750, and his 1752 schoolbook on "Forensic Disputes or Questions" is in the collection of the Yale University's Sterling Library. His handwriting was clear as he wrote down his positions on theological questions: "Should an innocent creature suffer pain?" or "Is There a God?" and "Witches, or Witch Stories." He argued for slavery in "Whether it Be Lawful to Make Negroes Slaves." On "Whether the Planets [are] Inhabited," he wrote on August 3, 1752, that "there is no ladder long enough to reach 'em," and "if you had disputed whether the moon is made of green Chese there had been some sense in it—but this is so sily I'll say no more about it."

Justus Forward graduated from Yale College in 1754 and settled as pastor of Belchertown, Massachusetts, in 1756. He later wrote in his diary about his parents' initial reluctance to see him go to Yale but that he had a "godly

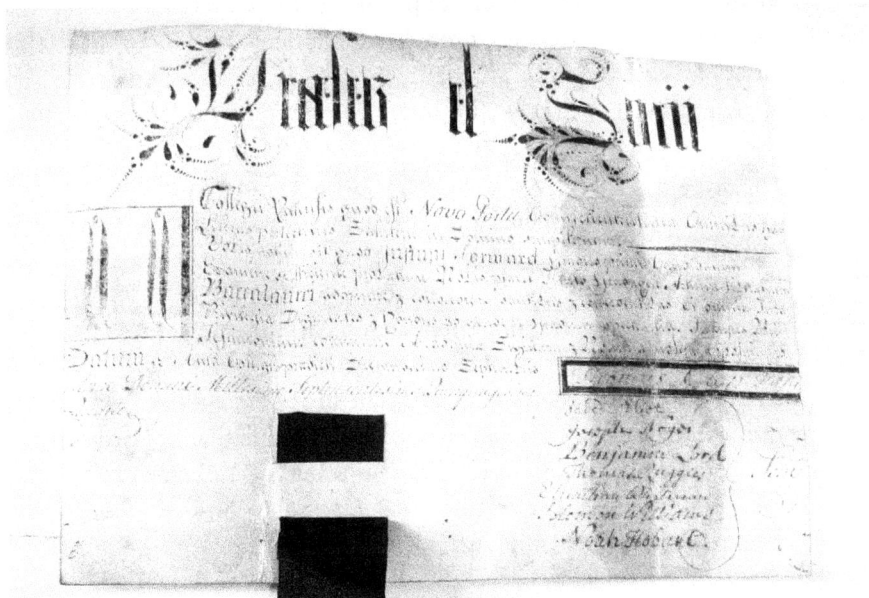

Yale College diploma (1754) of Reverend Justus Forward (1730–1814) of Turkey Hills (today East Granby), Connecticut, signed by president Thomas Clap. Reverend Forward was pastor of Belchertown, Massachusetts, from 1756 to 1814 and Reverend Rufus Hawley's cousin and mentor. This diploma resembled the one Rufus Hawley received after his one year at Yale, 1766–67. *Collection of the Stone House Museum, Belchertown, Massachusetts. Photograph by the author.*

and learned education and many pious counsels" and "God has honored me by employing me in his service."

When Rufus Hawley turned sixteen years old in 1757, his sister Abigail was thirteen and Deborah was ten. His brother Thomas was twenty-six, and Jesse was nineteen. The biggest crisis in Rufus's young life occurred that year with Jesse's death. His headstone honors him as a "Student." Rufus would follow his brother's scholarly example, with encouragement from Justus Forward and, presumably, the pastors of Salmon Brook (Joseph Strong Sr.) and Turkey Hills (Nehemiah Strong).

Three years after this, Timothy Hawley made plans to provide for his son Rufus, a young man destined not to become a farmer. Thomas already had received two hundred acres (most of his father's land), along with a house next door to his father's house, a barn and a five-acre farm. There was no provision for Rufus to inherit any farm in Turkey Hills, but Timothy arranged for Rufus to one day inherit 100 pounds, a sum equal in value to Thomas's land.

Rufus was on his way to becoming a pastor. Justus would write almost ten years later that young Rufus's desire to become a minister led him to "seek for a learned education (and to go through such difficulties in order to obtain it, as but few would have surmounted)."

In 1762, Rufus lived for weeks with Justus Forward and his family on their Belchertown farm, popping in and out of Justus's diary. Reverend Forward was teaching other young men that year, and it is almost certain that he was teaching Rufus. Justus paid Rufus, perhaps to help with the farm and the other students. Attending the Belchertown church during his visit and seeing Justus Forward at work, Rufus experienced the life of a pastor in a community of about three hundred people in sixty families—similar to what awaited him in his future parish of Northington.

On or about October 18, 1762, Rufus left his home in Turkey Hills to prepare for college at a school in Massachusetts called the Academy at Hatfield. He was probably about six feet tall, robust, with brown hair, blue eyes and an aquiline nose, features his sons would have in common. Rufus Hawley began his first surviving journal a few months later.

2

OUR LITTLE COLLEDGE

Hatfield, Massachusetts, 1763–1766

1763

The Gregorian calendar was adopted in 1752. Rufus Hawley followed this new calendar, adding eleven days to his birth date of February 21. Under the new calendar, he (usually) considered his birthday to be March 4.

JANUARY 1 Saturday fair but Something Cold

FEBRUARY 20 DD Snowd hard all Day and the Snow fell about a foot deep, went to Chh and it is now with what has fallen before I beliuve Four feet deep upon the [--]—for it never was So deep before Since my Rememberrance—And I am this Day 22 years old.

MARCH 4 Fryday fair and thaw'd; and I went to Hampton for a Slay ride in Company with Diggins, Dwight & both the Graves—This Day I am 22 years old.

Rufus Hawley, twenty-one, made his first entry in his new journal on New Year's Day 1763: "Saturday fair but Something Cold." On the cover, he had carefully written, "Rufus Hawley Ejus Ephemeris—Annoque Domini 1763." His "DD" symbol every Sunday stood for *Dies Domini*, or the Lord's Day. For his daily weather reports, he searched for just the right word: "fair," "exceeding rainy," "a Storming," "moderate for the season," "extream hot," "cool," "Something cool," "cold," "very cold," "extream cold" and "raw cold." It "haild," "haild hard," "Snowd," "thawd," "began to storm," "raind some," "raind Very hard" and "clear'd off pleasant." Days were "windy," "very windy," "violent," "blustering," "cloudy," "very pleasant" and "warm." There was a "remarkable Shower of rain," "a storm of rain and Thunder and Litening," an "extream tedious storm" and "a hard storm." A "February snowstorm," the deepest "since my Rememberrance," brought the depth of snow at the school to four feet.

Rufus arrived in Hatfield at the time of a religious revival in western Massachusetts. The pastor of Hatfield, Reverend Timothy Woodbridge (Yale, 1732), had opened the academy in 1762 and was its head; the center of the school's activities was his meetinghouse. The building was fifty-six feet long and forty-five feet wide; large square pews had high backs, and seating galleries were on either side of the upper floor. Stairs led to the high pulpit, and a sounding board amplified voices. It was in the Hatfield meetinghouse that students attended church services, ceremonies, Wednesday public lectures and Friday lectures "prepatory to the Sacrement" of Sunday's communion.

In order to prepare for college, the students at Hatfield studied logic, recitation, natural philosophy, rhetoric, oratory, ethics, theology, Hebrew, Greek and Latin. They learned to write essays, made oral presentations (called declaiming) and practiced debating (called disputing). By June 1763, the academy

Rufus Hawley's journal cover, 1763. "Revised in 1856" was an annotation by Edward Eugene Hawley, who transcribed parts of his grandfather's journals in 1856. *Hawley-August Collection, Avon Free Public Library. Photograph by John Pecora.*

had almost twenty students. The tutors were all Yale educated; along with Reverend Woodbridge, there was Reverend Jonathan Lyman (1758), Reverend Ebenezer Baldwin (1763) and Simeon Olcott (1761), a future senator from New Hampshire.

When the name of academy tutor Justus Forward appears in Rufus's journal, the question is answered as to how a Connecticut farm boy came to this elite Massachusetts school. Reverend Forward taught at the academy and lived just seventeen miles away in Belchertown. Slender, of medium stature, courteous and social, Justus Forward helped many young men prepare for college. Justus had started keeping a journal in 1752, during his time at Yale, and he taught Rufus this lifelong practice. Their journals are identical in size and style, right down to a hand and finger pointing to important entries.

The first Hatfield friend of whom Rufus wrote was Jonathan Dwight, followed by Augustus Diggins of East Windsor, Samuel Partridge of Hatfield and Justus Forward's young son Joshua. The academy allowed its students amusing diversions. Rufus "plaid Ball" on a pleasant April day in 1763, went swimming twice in the Mill River and saw two house raisings. He gathered strawberries in June and whortleberries in August. He walked to Hadley, two miles away, and with friends visited Belchertown and Hampton.

Three times that year, Rufus went home for school breaks. Traveling the thirty miles between Hatfield and Turkey Hills was a one-day journey, and it

Reverend Justus Forward, pastor of Belchertown, Massachusetts, wrote "Justus Forward Jany 18. 1763" on his Bible (Edinburgh, UK: Richard Watkins, 1747). *Collection of the Stone House Museum, Belchertown, Massachusetts. Photograph by the author.*

took two days if he stopped overnight at Salmon Brook or Belchertown. If traveling on a Sunday, he attended meetinghouse services wherever the day found him. For two weeks' vacation in the spring, after Uncle Abel Forward fetched him from school in a sleigh, he visited around home. His father Timothy then rode with him back to school, returning to Turkey Hills with his son's horse. When the academy school year ended on August 30, after exams by Reverend Woodbridge and Reverend Forward, Rufus went home for the September "vacancy." Miss Strong of Salmon Brook made him a gown—probably Martha Strong, age eighteen, the sister of Salmon Brook's pastor, Joseph Strong.

Rufus's second academy year began on October 3, 1763, and heading back to Hatfield, he wrote "facere aliquot negotium"—time to go back to work. From this point on, his custom on New Year's Eve would be to pick up his pen, dip it in black ink and write a final thought. That Saturday night, he dutifully concluded his first journal in a way that would have pleased his parents, his tutors and Justus Forward: "The year being now passed away and the new begins on the Lords Day."

1764

February 16 Thursday fair and Quite warm; Studied and I broke throug the ice in the Mill River and fell in up to my Arms &c.

September 10 Munday fair & Cool Came back as far as Westfield and Noble Set out with Me in order to go to Newhaven to Commensment, we Came to Fathers and past on to Farmington the same [--].

In Rufus Hawley's second year at the academy, one of his pleasures was walking across the frozen river to Hadley. After a spell of moderate temperatures in February, and in what was very nearly the end of him, he "broke throug the ice in the Mill River and fell in up to my Arms." With tutors away one night at a lecture in Deerfield, the students took a break from studying and worship and spent the time "all in Play." This entry is the first of many that begins with Rufus drawing a hand and pointing finger, an alert to the reader that the passage is important: "The gloabs that David Billings got were this Day brought to our Little Colledge." He went to the funeral of Mrs. Lucias Allis, writing that the "Corps [corpse] Lookd the awfullest that I ever saw."

Rufus went home to Turkey Hills for the one-month vacation in late March and attended a meetinghouse Fast Day service of prayer, repentance and sermons. A few days later, he rode to Cider Brook in Northington on business with his father. Riding to New Haven in September through a soaking rain, he attended commencement at Yale College. The miserable weather continued: "Wensday Commensment Day but a Very rainy and went to See them take their Degrees." Not surprisingly, he returned home "very poorly with a Cold." This may have been the first Yale commencement he attended, an event that became a lifelong custom almost every September. This New Year's Eve, he did not have much to say: "Adiew to 1764."

1765

FEBRUARY 25 Munday fair & warm; studied and in the Evening about 10 o'clock died Mr. Abraham Morton who was Very aged; whom we have good Reason to believe is gone to the Realms of Bliss above.

JUNE 28 Fryday fair & hot; Studied, and Just night Joshua Forward (Son to the Revd Mr. Justus Forward) was drowned.

January ended with "one of the Coldest dais that ever was known in the Cuntry," and a warm Saturday in March offered a chance to break up ice. "Spent Considerable of the Day breaking up the Mill River," Rufus wrote, helping to smash the ice to ensure that water wheels in the river's mills would have a steady flow of water.

A frost on May 26 was a surprise; a fierce June thunderstorm astounded him. It was

the most remarkable that I ever knew with regard to the hail that fell, for there was a great deal that fell as big as hens Eggs and Some bigger, for the Scholars weighed one that weighed three ounces, and measured another that measured seven inches & a half in Circumference and it brake abundance of our glass, and destroyed abundance of grain in Town—Studied.

December brought the deepest snow he had ever known to fall at once, right up to his knees.

Attending funerals and taking exams was now routine. After the "Very aged" Mr. Abraham Morton's funeral, Rufus wrote, "We have good Reason to believe is gone to the Realms of Bliss above." On a pleasant day in April, the scholars faced about twenty "Clergy Men" in the meetinghouse and had their "first bublick [public] Examination." That afternoon, two to three hundred people heard two orations, and Rufus participated in a public "Dispute."

April break began the day after exams. At home in Turkey Hills, doing chores with his father and sister Deborah, Rufus built a "bee house," visited waterfalls, sheared sheep and had clothes made by Elizabeth Post of Salmon Brook. During a round-trip journey of four days to New Haven with Deborah and Uncle Abel Forward, Rufus may have gone about gaining admission to Yale. For the Connecticut General Election in May, a day of sociability, he "rode over the mountain to see our friends."

School resumed in May with "recitations" and "disputing & Declaiming" in the meetinghouse. Then, on a fair and hot Friday in June, tragedy struck those he loved most. Joshua Dickinson Forward, age seven, drowned at Hatfield. The next day, Rufus rode home to "Tirkey hills to Carry the news" of the accidental loss of the only son of Reverend Justus and Violet Forward, writing that he was "overcame with my Jurney so that I Could not

The headstone of Joshua Forward (1757–1765), son of Reverend Justus and Violet Forward, in South Cemetery, Belchertown, Massachusetts. After young Joshua drowned, Rufus Hawley went to Belchertown to be with the Forward family. *Photograph by the author.*

Study." Two days after Joshua's death, family members and friends flocked to Hatfield for the funeral.

The weather stayed hot, and Rufus stayed frozen in his studies. Grief-stricken, he managed to attend church that Sunday and go fishing. July passed in the journal with few comments other than the weather, fishing, walking and exercising, but finally he "plaid Some." In August, after three days in Belchertown, he returned to school in time to visit with his sisters, Abigail, twenty-one, and Deborah, nineteen, who were going on to Belchertown to comfort the Forward family.

A year later, Reverend Justus Forward wrote poignantly in his diary of always desiring to serve God, even though his ministry was marked by trials, difficulties and the death of his only son. Rufus was not done grieving this year. The next month brought "news of the death of Elijah Graves, who was once my classmate." Characteristically, he wrote no more about it. A month later, he learned of the death of cousin Esther Hawley, about seventeen, of Farmington.

Finally, there was happiness: the Hatfield students had a public examination in the meetinghouse, and Rufus wrote with satisfaction that he "performed well" as a "multitude of people" watched. Back home in Turkey Hills for October break, he attended church, picked corn and cut cornstalks and went to Hatfield to return a horse. After losing loved ones this year, he wrote of his Hatfield friends with relief, saying he "found them well."

Although his academy studies were not finished, Rufus rode to Amherst, Massachusetts, in mid-October to secure a six-month teaching job. After the school committee "agre[ed] with me about keeping School," his brother Thomas helped him move to Amherst. Thomas was good company and could also take Rufus's horse back to Turkey Hills. As they rode through the snowy landscape, conversation perhaps turned to politics, for England would enact the Stamp Act in a few weeks. The dreaded stamps required on almanacs, newspapers, pamphlets, broadsides, legal documents, licenses, ship's papers and even playing cards meant rising expenses, taxation without representation in Parliament and possibly war.

1766

MAY 19 Munday fair & hot & in the Evening thunderd & raind some; this Day there is Publick rejoicing at Newhaven on the account of the Stamp Act's being repeald; but I Came from Newhaven with Sister we got as far as unkel Abel Hawley's of Meriden & there Lodged.

*September 28 DD fair & hot; rode to Belchers Town to Dwight's Funeral,
Six other Scholars went with Me: I was one of the Bearers; went to Chh.*

When Rufus's Amherst teaching job ended in April, he headed home for a month. Finding a warm reception with attentive Connecticut ministers, he seemed thrilled to attend the April ordination at the North Windsor meetinghouse of Theodore Hinsdale (Yale, 1762). At the invitation of Reverend Hinsdale, he dined with the council of ministers at the home of Reverend Hezekiah Bissell (Yale, 1733), pastor of Wintonbury (today Bloomfield). He then rode home to Turkey Hills with Reverend John Smalley (Yale, 1756) of New Britain and Reverend Joseph Strong (Yale, 1772) of Salmon Brook. Perhaps they discussed Rufus's imminent enrollment at Yale College.

In Turkey Hills, Rufus watched at the bedside of his dying uncle Joseph Forward, the father of Reverend Justus Forward. He also got a close view of church disharmony. At a two-day Hartford North Association meeting, the ministers examined the dispute Turkey Hills was having with its pastor, Reverend Nehemiah Strong. Visiting Yale on May 19 with his sister Deborah, Rufus saw the "publick rejoicing at Newhaven on the account of the Stamp Acts being repeald." On a colony-wide day of thanksgiving on May 23, bells in Hartford pealed and cannons blasted a twenty-one-gun salute.

Rufus took his last exams at the academy in June. Standing before Reverend Woodbridge, the scholars and the tutors, Rufus gave a speech on the recent death of Hatfield tutor Reverend Jonathan Lyman. Four days later, the students had public examinations in front of "a very Large Assembly of People." Reverend Ebenezer Baldwin and Samuel Partridge gave speeches, and there was a dispute in English and one in Latin. The next step was commencement, and in July, Rufus's classmates chose him to be the commencement orator. Immediately falling ill, he wrote "poorly all Day, & in the Evening I had Several fits, which I Sepose was cramp Convulsion Fits; very bad...I am yet very week." He had three months to prepare his speech.

Hatfield tutor Reverend Ebenezer Baldwin attended the Yale commencement in September and brought back the astounding news of the resignation of Thomas Clap, president for twenty-one years. It was the culmination of several months of near-rioting at Yale about the harsh discipline imposed by the president, with tutors resigning and disruptive students being absent from prayers. In his final valedictory address, Reverend Clap had spoken in Latin of his desire to "enjoy the Sweets of Retirement and private life," praying "that this College may yet flourish, and especially that the Religion of it may be preserved pure to the latest Generations."

The Journals of Rufus Hawley, Avon, Connecticut

On the afternoon of September 27, Rufus heard that Jonathan Dwight, about twenty-two years old and the first friend of whom he wrote in his journal, had died after sunrise at home in Belchertown. Reverend Justus Forward wrote in his diary that Jonathan had "returned from commencment ill & had the long fever of which he died, probally it was bilious too." Learning of the death of his academy and Yale classmate, Rufus and six other students immediately hastened to Belchertown to be with Jonathan's family. Earlier in the year, Rufus had visited Jonathan at his home and ominously remarked in the journal that Jonathan had left Yale "for the season."

Of this loss, Rufus wrote nothing more. Ten days later, on a cool and fair October day, he completed his studies at the academy with a public ceremony of examinations and disputes, Josiah Wilder's speech in Latin and his own valedictory address in English. The students received words of advice and were told to mind their manners. Justus Forward wrote in his diary that "Woodbridge, Wilder, Noble, Houghton, Partridge, Hawley were about to leave the school in order to perfect their studies at Yale College." Rufus's parents did not attend the academy ceremony, but Thomas Hawley was there and brought his brother a horse to ride home.

Rufus left for Turkey Hills the next day, going home "to Daddy's" with Thomas and their friend from Norwich, Thomas Huntington (Yale, 1768). During the brief two weeks before college, Anna Phelps of Turkey Hills made Rufus a jacket, and he returned to Hatfield to sell his cattle. The academy at Hatfield closed four years later, in 1770, having educated a total of only fifty to seventy students.

With his academy training behind him and through Justus Forward's influence, Rufus Hawley possessed a conservative Calvinist and Old Light education. His studies in Hatfield, Farmington, Turkey Hills and Belchertown would now culminate in one year at Yale.

3

A Pleasant Quarter

Yale College, 1766–1767

Autumn 1766

October 8 Wednesday fair & Cool; & we had a publick Examination, & in the afternoon some Collegiac Performances; (viz) a Silogistick & phorensick Dispute, & three Orations, one of which was a valedictory oration which I deliver'd, &c.

October 25 Saturday fair & pleasant; rode to New-haven, ariv'd there about Noon, & in the afternoon was examin'd with Houghton Wilder & Partridge in order to enter the Senior Class.

Rufus Hawley, age twenty-five, began his year at Yale College on a rainy Friday in October. "Set out on a Journey to New-haven [and] rode as far as Meriden & there Slept." Even though the weather turned fair and pleasant when he arrived the next day at noon, it was a dreadful time to begin college. Families had been withdrawing their sons, worried about unraveling school discipline and the political situation with England. By the spring of 1767, Yale had only about fifty students, and Rufus's senior class of twenty-four students was half the size of the senior class two years earlier.

Yale's problems were not evident in the journal, for Rufus seemed to make the best of being there with his good friends Augustus Diggins, Samuel Partridge, Josiah Wilder and Israel Houghton. The college at that time had four buildings. The only one remaining today is Connecticut Hall (1753), made of brick and three stories high, with bedrooms and study rooms. Today, it is a National Historic Landmark.

Yale College, built in 1718 (taken down in stages between 1775 and 1782), was three stories high. It had clapboards painted sky blue, an attic, six chimneys and a bell in the belfry. The ground floor had a chapel, a kitchen and a large Great Hall dining room, or Commons. The library above the Great Hall had four thousand books on history, divinity, philosophy, medicine, science, literature and mathematics. There were works by William Shakespeare, Isaac Newton, John Locke, Geoffrey Chaucer, John Milton and Francis Bacon. Tutors used scientific instruments to teach about the divine hand in the natural world: globes, a reflecting telescope, surveying instruments, a small astronomical quadrant, a compound microscope, a barometer, a thermometer, a theodolite and an electrical machine. There were sleeping rooms, each suitable for two or three students, with small closets for quiet study. Some students, like Rufus, lived with New Haven landlords.

The third building at Rufus Hawley's time was the chapel (demolished in 1893), fifty feet by forty feet, with a library on the third floor and galleries on the second floor for orations and disputations. The fourth building was the college president's house, built in 1721.

Upon arrival at Yale, Rufus immediately sat for his Greek and Latin exams, writing that he was "examin'd with Houghton, Wilder and Partridge in order to enter the Senior Class." The next day he went to chapel services for "the first time." Exams continued on Monday when "we were examin'd again all day & admitted to the Senior Class." When he returned briefly to Turkey Hills, he found a wagon "to Carry my things" to New Haven and took two days to get back to Yale, with an overnight stop in Farmington. Uncle Abel Forward (Yale, 1768), Aunt Hannah Forward and their son Abel, eighteen, accompanied Rufus to New Haven. After saying their farewells, Rufus made "preparations for living at Mr Colemans," where he shared a room with at least one other scholar. He wrote in his journal of taking his meals in the Commons.

One of Thomas Clap's last acts as president had been to assign each incoming student a permanent class rank, according to the student's social status. This custom meant that Rufus ate, sat in class and participated in academic exercises according to his rank as a farmer's son. Outranking him were the sons of political leaders and judges, sons of college graduates, sons of trustees, sons of ministers, sons of alumni and sons of wealth. Outranking him was almost everyone except for sons of storekeepers, mariners and artisans. Out of the senior class's twenty-four scholars, he was ranked twenty-third. Coming in last was his friend Augustus Diggins.

On a typical day, the Yale students rose at six o'clock in the morning, or when the light was sufficient, and attended morning prayers in the chapel. Breakfast and class followed, with a midmorning snack, a break and classes until lunch. Free time in the afternoon (one and a half hours) was followed by study, class and late afternoon prayers. After supper, students were at leisure until study time, from 9:00 p.m. to 11:00 p.m. Their studies included rhetoric, oratory, ethics, theology, reciting, disputing and declaiming, grammar, language and composition. Rufus undoubtedly practiced public speaking and how to follow an extemporaneous sermon outline. Tutor Jonathan Trumbull described the students as condemned each day to study, read, recite and pray; his description applied partially to Sunday as well, a day of prayer.

In November, sick with a severe cold and fever that lasted ten days, Rufus barely managed to take his exams. "My Class was examin'd; my self not well, yet attended Examination." Dr. Leverett Hubbard gave Rufus "a Vomit which operated thouroughly." On Dr. Hubbard's second visit, he "Spake no wise comforting for he said I had Something of the Long Fever, he Left some medicens for me & I went to Mr Colemans & began to take them; upon which I felt a Little better & My Fever abated." Vastly improved and cheerful a week later, Rufus wrote "a pleasant Quarter we have had."

New Year's Eve was memorable for the "extream Cold" of twenty-five degrees, the coldest recorded temperature "Since Experiments have been made at Yale College." Three months at Yale had passed quickly: "Oh how fleeting is Time."

1767

JULY 8 Wednesday fair & moderate: Sail'd to Long isleland with a Number of Scholars & Ladies; I was very Sick the wind was against us so that we Could not get to the Place we aim'd at the first Day, but just into the Harbour Cal'd the Old mans where we tarried all Night.

SEPT 9 Wednesday fair & warm: This Day is Comminsment at New-haven, & I took the Degree of A.B. & We had a very Still peacable Comminsment & a fine Dance at Night; & every thing Consider'd it is Said by the People in general to be one of the Grandest Comminsments that ever was at Yale.

The controversial and obstinate Reverend Thomas Clap, sixty-four, died in January. Inclined to never write ill of people, Rufus called him "wise & Learned," recording after his funeral that "this Day was inter'd the Remains of President Clap." Another Yale student, not so kind, scribbled in a Yale library book, "Tomme Clap you Fool do not think that I mind your Finis."

Shortly after this, back home for almost two months, Rufus found there was "no Preaching at Turkey hills," and for an astonishing reason: Reverend Nehemiah Strong's church was in such "uneasiness" that the society had delivered seven charges against him to the Hartford North Association of ministers. There had been financial disagreements and the loss of church members to a nearby Church of England, but the pastor's personal life caused the biggest stir.

Reverend Strong's wife, Mrs. Lydia Smith Burr Strong, had once been granted a divorce for desertion by her first husband, Mr. Burr. But the wayward Mr. Burr returned for his wife, the General Assembly annulled the divorce and Lydia left Reverend Strong for Mr. Burr. It was just too much for Turkey Hills. Although the Hartford North Association dismissed the charges against Reverend Strong, it could not reconcile the pastor and his people. Rufus attended a three-day meeting in February with the "advisory council," and the Turkey Hills Society voted to dismiss Reverend Strong. There would be no settled pastor in Turkey Hills for six more years.

After Yale's "Quarter Examination" in June, Rufus found time for leisure. Spending three days and two nights on Long Island Sound with "a Number of Scholars & Ladies," he sailed across the sound to the North Shore of Long Island. The carefree group spent the night in Old Man's Harbor (Mount Sinai, Long Island) and sailed to Setauket, where it spent the second night. Rufus grew seasick in the strong winds but enjoyed the adventure. It stands out in all his journals as a singular moment when he was on unfamiliar waters, blown off course, separated from responsibilities, young, single and unchaperoned.

Back at Yale, work awaited as he prepared for the final exam required for his college degree. After the speeches in the chapel on exam day, the moderator put the prospective graduates' statuses to a vote. "Wednesday we were examin'd for Degrees, intitl'd to the Same: the Day was Cloudy & rain'd Some, & my horse Came."

With one and a half months until commencement in September, Rufus rode home by way of Farmington and stayed the night with classmate John Treadwell. The pride of Turkey Hills arrived home to find he was desperately needed in the absence of a settled pastor. He led the Sunday service, but his leadership was limited without a preaching license. "Read all Day, & made one Prayer," he wrote. Needing to move his belongings from Yale, he searched for three days and found a wagon and a horse in Simsbury "to fetch my things from New haven."

He found time to plow, mow, meet up with Yale classmates Amos Butler and Charles Kellogg, visit Justus Forward in Belchertown and go twice to West Simsbury (today Canton Center) to hear preaching by pastor Reverend Gideon Mills (Yale, 1737). Reverend Mills's daughter Elizabeth, about thirteen years old, must have been in the family pew. In time, the paths of Elizabeth and Rufus would cross again.

As Yale College's commencement drew near, Justus and Violet Forward arrived at Turkey Hills. Justus intended to go on to New Haven for the ceremony, but his health prevented him from going any farther. Suffering from nephritic colic, a kidney ailment with back pain and vomiting, Justus called off "my journey to Newhaven as I found it would worry me." He must have been deeply disappointed.

Rufus left home for commencement on September 7 with his sister Abigail Hawley, Justus's brother Joseph Forward and Lieutenant Zaccheus Gillet. After he arrived in New Haven on the eve of the ceremony, he "got things in Order." Spectacular fireworks lit up the night sky, and the "largest lumination that ever was at the college" was thrilling.

The weather stayed warm and fair for commencement two days later. With ministers and lay people in attendance, Reverend Naphtali Daggett opened the ceremony with prayer and delivered a speech about the late president, Thomas Clap. Then, each graduate spoke on his thesis and received his degree. Rufus wrote only that "this Day is Comminsment at New-haven, & I took the Degree of A.B. [bachelor of arts] and We had a very Still, peaceable Comminsment & a fine Dance at Night; & everything Consider'd, it is said by People in general to be one of the Grandest Comminsments that ever was at Yale."

The new Yale graduate undoubtedly felt the responsibility of his privileged education. Rufus's college classmates, mostly from Connecticut with a few from Massachusetts and New York, would become General Assembly representatives, doctors, farmers, teachers, traders, tavern keepers and Patriot or Loyalist fighters in the American Revolution. John Treadwell of Farmington became governor of Connecticut and the founder of the American Board of Commissioners for Foreign Missions. John Trumbull worked for John Adams and became a Connecticut Superior Court judge. Approximately 29 percent of the class (seven men) became pastors.

Awaiting a call from a church society to be its settled pastor, Rufus, twenty-six, sought a teaching job and worried about his "unwell" cousin Rachel Forward, seventeen. Captain Abel Forward hoped his daughter would benefit from being near the sea air of Long Island Sound. Ever helpful, Rufus took Rachel to East Haven, fifty miles from Turkey Hills, to stay at the home of East India trade merchant Captain Amos Morris. The wait began "to See what effect the Sea Air had on Rachel." At home in Turkey Hills after his journey, Rufus did chores, mowed hay and stored it in the barn, hunted, studied and tried to find pastors to come and preach in the meetinghouse on Sundays.

After five weeks in East Haven, Rachel's alarming condition prompted her father to bring her home. Rufus met them in Farmington, where he found Rachel "vastly more poorly" and unable to sit in a carriage. "We got a Chair, but Rachel Could not bear to ride in it, then got a Horse cart & put a Bed therein with which we brought her softly home." Rufus attended church the following Thursday, November 19, for the traditional "publick Thanksgiving in Connecticut." From there, he immediately went to keep watch at Rachel's, where she died four days later. In his longest journal passage yet, he wrote:

> *About 3 OClock in the Morning I was Call'd to take a Last Look & farewell of Rachel Forward who they Sepos'd was then a Dying, but by indulgent Heaven reviv'd & Continu'd till after Nine; then She Left the World with the greatest Calmness Serenity & Composure; having previously Caution'd & warn'd her Brothers & Sisters all around her to forsake Sin & follow the ways of Virtue; & having expresd a willingness to Die & even a Desire therefore, Likewise takeing her Leave of her Parents in the melting expressions following! Dear Parents farewell, after which She (as we have the greatest Reason to believe) fell asleep in Jesus.*

Rufus quickly set his mind elsewhere. A few days after Rachel's death, he rode from Turkey Hills "over the Mountain to a Library meeting," the first journal entry about what became a lifelong interest. Still awaiting his call to a parish, he boarded in Suffield and taught at the town's new schoolhouse six days a week. Dwight Lyman, his academy friend from Suffield, stopped to visit. Did Rufus know that if war came, Dwight would fight for Great Britain? What Rufus certainly knew was that brothers, classmates and cousins could die suddenly. His gratitude on New Year's Eve was not for his elite education at Hatfield or Yale, or even about his hopes for his future: "Thanks to God for Sparing My Life another Year."

4

THEY CHOSE ME FOR THEIR MINISTER

Northington, 1768–1769

1768

JULY 12 Tuesday fair & hot: began to Study, & to compose a Sermon on Rom. 5.19. it being the first that ever I compos'd

NOVEMBER 2 Wednesday Cloudy & a very rainy afternoon: they continu'd my Examination, & I read my common-place Sermon (which was rote on Rom. 8.3) & about Noon they gave me a Sertificate licenceing me to preach as a Candidate for the Gospel Ministry; there was a publick Lector, attended it.

Rufus's time was well spent in Suffield, where he attended church and had the customary teaching job appropriate for a future pastor. He also became better acquainted with Miss Deborah Kent, twenty-nine, who lived with her brother John in Suffield. Deborah had professed her faith in her youth and was accustomed to having ministers in the family. Grandfather Benjamin Ruggles (Harvard, 1693) had been Suffield's first pastor, and other relatives had been pastors of Simsbury, Groton and Wethersfield and of Newtown, Massachusetts.

In May, Rufus and Deborah went on a weeklong visit to New Haven. The weather was rainy and windy, so instead of sailing, they "spent the Day walking & going into the College Library." It was a peaceful interlude before returning to Suffield, where his teaching job was in jeopardy.

A Mr. Pease had turned a disagreement with Rufus into a reason to put a new man into the job. Rufus's supporters rose up and evicted the new schoolmaster. "Miss Deborah & I return'd to Suffield; but to my surprise my Place was Supply'd, for Mr. Pease on some slight affront with me had put Kellogg into the School; but it was so disagreeable to the People that they got together at Night & turn'd him out, So that his Reign was but one Day." A month later, however, Mr. Pease won the upper hand. Rufus dismissed school "at Noon because of Some Dificulties occation'd by Pease." After gathering his "Cloaths" and settling his affairs, he "bid farewell to Suffiel'd" and returned to Turkey Hills.

During this unsettled time in his life, Rufus kept visible to other pastors and congregations. Suffield's Reverend Ebenezer Gay Sr. (Harvard, 1737) invited him to dine. In Hartland, he joined with other pastors and friends on a knoll to celebrate the ordination of Reverend Sterling Graves (Yale, 1765).

He also prepared to take exams for his preaching license, spending a month in Belchertown living and studying with Justus Forward. Under Justus's eye, Rufus spent four days writing his first sermon: "Began to Study, & to compose a Sermon on Rom. 5.19. it being the first that ever I compos'd." The second day was spent "in composition," and the next day he studied. On the fourth day, he "Studied, & finish'd my Sermon" on a scripture passage about one man's example making many people righteous. With this very first sermon completed, Rufus spent eight days writing answers to theological questions and wrote on July 18 that he "studied & wrote in answer to Questions given me by the Rev'd Mr Forward in order to examination for preaching."

In early August, Rufus rode to Hadley, Massachusetts, to be examined for his license to preach. The exam, however, would have to wait, for there was trouble with one examiner, the suddenly single Reverend Nehemiah Strong, former pastor of Turkey Hills. Rufus wrote with dismay that "by the Advice of the Association & Some other reasons I defer'd it." With the exam delayed three months, he returned home and "studied faithfully." Listening to a guest pastor in Turkey Hills named Mr. Woster was a big disappointment. "I went to hear him, but did not like him." Rufus decided he was better off spending Sundays in Salmon Brook's meetinghouse or in Deborah Kent's Suffield meetinghouse. Come September, as always, he yearned to be in New Haven: "This Day is Comminsment at N. Haven."

In assembling a suitable wardrobe for a traveling pastor, Rufus had a Suffield tailor make a cloak for riding horseback through cold and wet weather. A cloak was usually made of wool broadcloth and required a large amount of fabric, so not surprisingly he went to Suffield more than once "to carry Some Cloath, not haveing eno for my cloak before." On that second visit to Suffield, Rufus and Deborah were clearly a couple. "Deacon Phelps Sent & invited the Groom & Bride [Samuel Phelps and Deborah's sister Lucy Kent Phelps], Mr John Kent & Miss Ruth, Miss Debbe & myself to come & Dine with him, we went."

In October, Rufus returned to the Forward farm in Belchertown to finish preparations for his licensing exam. Looking out the windows, he would have seen fields of flax, wheat, rye and hay. Sounds and smells of the bleating sheep, whinnying horses, mooing cows and snorting pigs must have drifted into the house. A few days later, Justus took Rufus to Hatfield, where they "attempted to Settle Some Difficulties between Mr. Strong & myself & in Some Measure accomplished it."

The critically important licensing exam by the Hampshire Association of ministers was November 1, in Northfield, Massachusetts, thirty-five miles north of Belchertown. This was a group of ministers extremely favorable to the young man. It was Justus Forward's association, and the ministers would have known Rufus Hawley from his days at Hatfield Academy. Rufus's journal does not mention Reverend Forward accompanying him to the exam.

That evening, Rufus faced the association's questions on languages, liberal arts, science and divinity, and the next day he delivered his "common-place" sermon from the book of Romans 8:8. On the third day of the examination, "about Noon they gave me a Sertificate licenceing me to preach as a Candidate for the Gospel Ministry; there was a publick Lector, attended it." A little more than a year after leaving Yale, Rufus, now twenty-seven, had passed his licensing exam and could now preach in any meetinghouse that would have him.

He began his ride home on November 3, traveling by way of Amherst and sleeping that night at the home of his former landlord, "old Mr. Coleman." In Belchertown the next day, he visited Captain Nathaniel Dwight, whose late son Jonathan had been Rufus's Hatfield friend.

On Sunday, November 6, Rufus preached for his first time as a certified minister. Summoning his courage, he went to the pulpit in Justus Forward's Belchertown meetinghouse. He "preach'd all Day for Mr Forward, & made the last Prayer a.m & the first pm, & was not much Scared although it was the first Time I ever preach'd." Heading home with Justus's mother, "Aunt Forward," and with "night coming on," they stopped in Suffield, where Deborah Kent presumably offered congratulations. His horse, anxious to get to Turkey Hills as soon as possible, made a break for it. "Our Horse got out of the Pasture & ran home in the night." Of his own return to Turkey Hills, he wrote only that he "came home to Fathers," but his happiness seemed evident in a whimsical journal entry four days later. A November day was "very pleasant over Head but very muddy under Feet."

Other pastors welcomed the new preacher and showed him off, having him preach at Turkey Hills, Windsor and Simsbury. Rufus was out and about, being seen and making it known that he needed his own parish. He may have had his eye on the vacant pulpit in Northington.

The parish of Northington, established in 1751, was the northern part of Farmington. Also known as an ecclesiastical society, the parish had been without a settled minister since early 1767, when Reverend Ebenezer Booge, fifty-one, had died unexpectedly fifteen years into his pastorate, leaving his widow, Damaris, and seven young children. He also left behind a tidy list of vital records from his time as pastor: 218 births, 260 baptisms, 58 marriages and 65 deaths.

Christopher Bickford, author of *Farmington*, points out that a community suffering the death of its pastor also suffered "a crisis of leadership and a breakdown of cohesion." With no time to lose, Northington immediately

Headstone of "ye late Prodent Pious & Faithful" Reverend Ebenezer Booge (1716–1767), Yale College (1748) and Avon's first pastor. Stone carving by Gershom Bartlett (1723–1798). Cider Brook Cemetery, Avon, Connecticut. *Photograph by Peter Wright, 2010.*

began searching for Reverend Booge's successor. Two weeks after the pastor's death, the society agreed to pay Damaris Booge for providing room and board to visiting ministers. A month after that, the society established a committee of Joseph Hart, Esq., Simeon Judd and Ensign William Woodford to call candidates to preach and to ask the Hartford North Association of ministers for advice.

Three newly licensed and Yale-educated ministers supplied the Northington pulpit: James Eells, Abner Johnson and Salmon Hurlbutt. Still, there was no settled pastor. In late November 1768, Rufus Hawley rode the fifteen miles from his home in Turkey Hills "to Northington on Business; & the Society's Committee being inform'd that I was in Town came two of them & desir'd me to come & preach with them the insuing Sabboth, I concluded to go, after wh I rode home."

The following Sunday, December 4, 1768, Rufus Hawley "preach'd att Northington & was the first Time that ever I preach'd there." The rain poured down that day. "Cloudy & about Noon began to rain & rain'd hard all the afternoon & considerable of the Night carried of chief of the Snow & made a Flood."

The society of Northington invited him back, and on a snowy Saturday a week later, Rufus rode from Turkey Hills to Northington to preach a second time. He then wrote that the committee "came to me & desir'd me to preach with them on probation—I took the Matter into Consideration, & was to give them an Answer in a few Days."

Rufus went home to Turkey Hills to make up his mind about the possibility of becoming pastor of Northington. He "did a few Chores, & made Preparations to go to Northington to Live, in order to preach there." After preaching for the third time in Northington two days later, he felt ready to commit the rest of his life to the parish. "They came this evening to receive my answer, which I gave them in the affirmative."

The candidate fell into the swirl of parish life. The church had him leave Timothy Thomson's house, where he had been living, and board at Damaris Booge's home. Visiting around the parish, he spent a day with Mary Hart Moss in labor and "exercis'd with Fits." The next day, he prayed with her and departed just before baby Mary was born. Mrs. Moss died that same evening. Participating in his first Northington funeral, he "made a prayer" at the home of Mrs. Moss's father, Joseph Hart, Esq.

It had been a long road from the Turkey Hills farm where he lost his brother Jesse, to the academy at Hatfield where he was guided and guarded by Reverend Justus Forward, to Yale College where he received a privileged education, to Massachusetts where he passed his preaching exams. On the verge of having his own parish, Rufus Hawley was grateful this New Year's Eve for two things:

*Thanks be to the Lord that
He has Spard my Life thro' another
year, & Shew'd me So many Favors.*

1769

MAY 22 Monday the Chh in Northington had a Meeting to see if they chose me for their Minister, they voted in ye Affirmative.

DECEMBER 7 DD Thursday fair & very pleasant. the Council met according to Adjurnment & brought in their result, which was to go on. And this day I was seperated to the work of the Ministry, & Ordained over the Chh & Congregation of Northington after which some of the Council set out for home

Rufus attended to the needs of Northington's approximately sixty families and fifty-eight church members. There were newborn twins at Sergeant David North's house, and with one infant "poorly," Sergeant North "sent this Evening for me to go & pray with it & them. I went & after haveing made a Prayer, went off to Mr Brunson's & lodged; but the Child died before Morning." The next day, he returned to pray shortly before the other twin's death. The two infants shared a coffin, and the pastor "made a Prayer with the Mourners" at the funeral.

After two days of snow followed by ten days of cold, the conditions were perfect for moving Ozias and Abigail Brownson's house on February 13. "Mr. Brunson had a House draw'd about half a Mile; went to see it draw'd, & it was done (Thro' god's Mercy) without any Body's being hurt, & without any great Damage to the house."

This was a year of firsts. Rufus preached in Northington almost every Sunday, leaving only for exchanges with five other pastors. On a Connecticut Fast Day, he preached all day "the first fast that ever I preach'd." He taught in the schoolhouses, visited house to house, paid calls on the sick and dined regularly with Deacon Ebenezer Miller. When his horse became ill, he found larch tree bark in a swamp to ease its sores and swellings.

On April 24, the society minutes recorded the vote to "grant Mr. Rufus Hawley for settlement with us in Northington in the gospel ministry." Rufus wrote that "the Society had a Meeting to see if they would Settle me as their Minister, they voted to Settle me & voted a Settlement & sallery & chose a Committee to come & inform me of their doings & to conduct their other affairs relative to Setling, they came & a number of other people wt them." Three weeks after the vote, the settlement was put in writing, and ordination plans kicked into high gear. The society selected June 28 for the ordination and alerted the tavern keepers. Rufus asked Reverend Justus Forward to deliver the ordination sermon.

There was trouble, however. When Rufus tried to meet with the Hartford North Association ministers for his ordination exam, they postponed the meeting for a week. He went to Stafford, about thirty miles from Northington, for the rescheduled meeting, but the association postponed that one too in order to move it to Northington "to enquire into affairs."

The Hartford North Association's council came to Northington soon after, examined him and licensed his ordination. Still, Rufus wrote, "some object against my settleing among them." He never said why, but perhaps his predicament was similar to the problems of Yale classmate Reverend Nathaniel Emmons in New Britain. Opposed by Harvard-educated Reverend Edward Eells of Cromwell for unsound doctrine, Reverend Emmons barely made it through his exams for a preaching license.

Rufus was right to be concerned. The opposing party formed a council to meet at Northington, and the committee ordered him to move from Mrs. Booge's house and board with society treasurer Ensign Cornelius Thomson and his wife. On what should have been his ordination day, he wrote that "the Party that oppos'd Settling would not submit the matter to them, so that the Council broke up & did nothing." A week later, the society set a new ordination date, Wednesday, August 9. Rufus held a Fast Day for the parish "on Account of my Setling in the Ministry among them," perhaps hoping that prayers and sacrifice might actually make the elusive ceremony take place.

Ordination day drew near. Pastors, friends, family and association officials arrived in Northington, and Reverend Justus Forward came from Belchertown. "[T]he people are very busy making preparations for my ordination which is to be on the Morrow: Mr. Forward & some others of the Council came this day." The next day, the spiritual and worldly lives of Rufus Hawley and his people would be officially joined for the rest of his life.

The journal entry for this next day, August 9, 1769, is astonishing. While Rufus's estimate of three thousand people in attendance seems high, this figure at least implies an immense crowd. His fears were realized on that hot day. "The rest of the Council came & heard & considered the objections made by an opposing Party & judged them insufficient to hinder the ordination: but yet all things consider'd they thought it not best for me to be ordained at present & so there was an End of the ordination & the large concourse of People, supposed to be about three thousand…dispers'd." The journal is silent on what went through Rufus's mind but is clear on what he did next. He left immediately for Suffield with Reverend Justus Forward and Deborah Kent's brother John.

Rufus preached in New Britain the next two Sundays. Perhaps seeking advice and peace, he visited friends in Middletown, Rocky Hill, Wethersfield and Windsor and then went fishing. Obliged to supply the Northington pulpit for two Sundays in September, he sent his friend Reverend Gideon Mills of West Simsbury (today Canton Center) and stayed in Suffield to preach for Reverend Ebenezer Gay Sr. While in Farmington with John and Elizabeth Hawley Newell, his uncle and aunt, the heavens opened up in August. "Most remarkable shower—it rained about an hour excessively hard & the ground seemed to be all afloat—the brooks rose and ran with such impetuosity that they washed away fences, tore away good stone bridges & beat down stone walls & tore the roads so much that the people were obliged to immediately go work on the highways in order that people might pass."

A week after the storm, on August 21, the society of Northington called him to be its pastor. He refused, writing in his journal that "this day the People of Northington had a Society Meeting & voted to continue their call to me & the committee came at evening to inform me of their doings; & in consequence of the advice I have taken I concended to withdraw for a season, & then if they continue united & invite me to return, to come back to them again."

Justus Forward may have been among those advising Rufus, for Justus arrived soon after his cousin withdrew from Northington. The two men visited at Thomas Hawley's farm in Turkey Hills and went fishing together. In September, before riding to the Yale commencement in September with Seth Lee of Farmington, Rufus stopped in Northington on his way to New Haven, and "several people came in to see me in the evening." After having been the target of indecision and unpleasantness in Northington, he wrote of a warm reception at Yale: "We put up at Capt Brindles, & after unbooting we walked down to college & were kindly received &c, there was a large Illumination & things went on well." A change at this commencement hinted at the seriousness of colonial political issues: the graduates' clothing was of homespun fabric, following Boston's 1769 Non-Importation Agreement forbidding the importation of almost everything from Great Britain, including textiles and tea. Rufus wrote only that commencement went well and was "conducted with regularity."

Northington refused to let the candidate go, so Rufus sought more advice. In late September, after the Northington committee sent Joseph Miller to ask Rufus Hawley to return as pastor, Rufus wrote that "[I] consulted with the [Hartford North] Association about settling at Northington, & they not advising me to it, I have concluded to leave, after preaching one Sabbath more with them." Perhaps the association had higher aspirations for this Yale graduate than settling in a small country parish.

During his farewell sermon in Northington on October 8, Rufus considered the possibility of being called again to settle, telling the story of a Roman governor who accused the apostle Paul of doing evil. The governor, said Rufus to those assembled, would call back Paul when it was convenient. In the Northington meetinghouse that Sunday "many of the people wept much," and four days later Rufus "pack'd up my Books & Cloaths & bid farewell to Northington, & rode home to Father's."

That first Sunday back with his parents, he preached in Turkey Hills, and Reverend Joseph Strong "much urge'd" him to preach in Salmon Brook. He soon learned that some ministers (he did not name them) had advised Northington to ordain him, writing in late October that people had been "encouraged to come & ordain me."

Ensign Cornelius Thomson, Rufus's former landlord in Northington, went to Turkey Hills to fetch Rufus Hawley and to plan one more time for his ordination. Mrs. Thomson and the tavern keepers began their preparations, but the day before the ordination, there was another delay. The council met and "hear'd the objections of a Party who opposed my setling, and examin'd me largely and publickly, and judged the objections insufficient, and judged me qualified for the Ministry & concluded to go on with the ordination: but night coming on, they adjurn'd till next morning & defer'd publishing their report till then." The ordination ground to a halt for a third excruciating time.

The next day, fair and pleasant, was Thursday, December 7, 1769, almost a full year since the candidate's first sermon in Northington. The moment for which Rufus had worked so diligently had arrived. "The Council met...& brought in their result, which was to go on," he wrote. "And this day I was seperated to the work of the Ministry, & ordained over the Chh & Congregation of Northington after which some of the Council set out for home." The church minutes recorded simply that "the Reverend Mr. Rufus

Reverend Rufus Hawley's journal, December 7, 1769, describing his ordination, which was held in what is today Avon. "Thursday fair & very pleasant. the Council met according to Adjurnment & brought in their Result, which was to go on. And this day I was seperated to the work of the Ministry, & Ordained over the Chh & Congregation of Northington after which Some of the Council set out for home." *Hawley-August Collection, Avon Free Public Library. Photograph by John Pecora.*

Hawley [was] ordained over the church & society of Northington in Farmington, to be their gospel minister." Rufus recorded that his sisters Abigail and Deborah attended the ordination but neglected to say that Reverend Justus Forward gave the ordination sermon. The original copy of the speech, a small document the size of the journals, is in the collection of Yale University. Justus Forward wrote on the cover that he gave "mostly" all the speech. Too long to finish before the large crowd on a warm day, the printed sermon runs more than forty pages. "My dear Kinsman," Justus said, asking for the congregation's patience, then addressed his cousin personally:

> *Since you are near to me by the ties of nature, blood and friendship; and since you began and for some time prosecuted your studies under my care, and especially since it is at your desire that I have undertaken to speak on this solemn occasion, permit me to speak freely to you... You will hardly spend any time more profitably for yourself and your people than that which you spend in your study; there you will meditate on things of the greatest importance to yourself and them.*

Justus Forward publicly warned Rufus Hawley of his grave responsibilities: "I hope, and pray...that he and you may be mutual blessings to, and mutually blessed in and with each other for a long time to come in this world, and that you may meet and rejoice together forever in a better world." And then, as Rufus said later after a colleague's ordination, "the solemnity was over." People offered congratulations and made their way home or to a tavern for celebration and dancing.

A few days later, Rufus rode with Justus Forward to Suffield, where they parted. Justus had to get home to Belchertown; as for Rufus, Deborah Kent was in Suffield, and he was not due back in Northington for a few days.

Two weeks after his ordination, Rufus gave his first sermon in Northington as settled pastor, pledging his lifelong service and leadership. But there were also personal matters to attend to, such as building his first house. On a cold day, he "spent the afternoon viewing land," and as the year closed, there was another first: he "preach'd & baptiz'd Asahel, son to Ozias Brownson, which was the first child that ever I baptiz'd."

Northington had its new pastor. A relieved and perhaps surprised Reverend Rufus Hawley finally had his parish. He was grateful on New Year's Eve:

> *Many & great have been the*
> *favours of God to me this year: [--]*
> *bless the Lord o my soul.*

5

Unspeakable Gifts

The Settled Pastor, 1770–1775

1770: No Journal

The society paid Reverend Hawley a settling bonus in cash and land, valued at 150 pounds. The catch, however, assured his long-term commitment to Northington; if ever his behavior led to his dismissal, he must return this sum. His annual salary was one-third cash (received at year's end) and two-thirds donated labor and products, such as flax, wheat, hay, turnips, wood, pork, fish and the ending corn of the season for making cornmeal. Every year, he also received seventeen and a half cords of free wood, and after six years, he would receive twenty cords, which was enough for the cooking and heating needs of a small house.

During this first summer as pastor, perhaps he looked into the night sky to see Lexell's comet pass over Northington. The *Connecticut Courant* said that the moonlight and sunlight diminished the comet's "illustrious appearance" and "true luster." Northington's new pastor, on the other hand, was clearly visible. He assisted the sick and injured, witnessed wills and taught religion to promising boys. Rufus visited Northington's children in their homes, schoolhouses and meetinghouse and heard the children recite answers to his religious questions. "Catechis'd the Children at the meetinghouse p.m.," he wrote in July, and "there were 84 present." Preaching to people gathered in one another's homes was routine. His son, Timothy, would write later that his father led the congregation with "a strict regard for duty." The parish's vital records reveal many of his duties and concerns in 1770: sixteen births, twenty baptisms, three weddings and five deaths.

The Northington meetinghouse, built in 1754, was located near the Farmington River at what is today the west end of the street called Reverknolls, off Route 10. Like the typical Connecticut meetinghouse, its interior was probably not pristine. Men in church chewed and spat tobacco, and apple cores and nutshells might be on the floor. Mice, dogs, chickens, insects, birds and bats entered through doors, holes and windows. Snow, ice, dust, dirt and smoke came in as well. The only housekeeping mentioned in the Northington church minutes was the monthly sweeping.

Sunday services were in the morning and afternoon, and the pastor expected every able-bodied person, church member or not, to attend both. The congregation, in turn, expected to hear him give two new sermons every Sunday, and he always wrote in the journal which Scripture passages he used. To write sermons, Rufus "mused and wrote" and said his "business was Studying." The journals never say how long it took to write a new sermon, but a comparison can be made to the seven hours it took Cotton Mather of Boston to write a new sermon, reading the Bible in its original languages, studying Bible commentaries and praying.

When circumstances made it impossible for him to write a new sermon, he delivered an old one. There were plenty of reasons for being unprepared: pressing chores, a new baby, a tragedy or someone letting him down. "Being disappointed of Help[,] which I expected[,] I preach'd old sermons." Sometimes it was too cold to think or write. After a frigid week when the congregation failed to deliver his wood, he preached "old Sermons because I had no Wood to keep a Fire in my Study."

The Bible in the Northington pulpit was likely the King James version, the English translation of the Bible used in Protestant churches at the time. Standing before his congregation, Rufus delivered sermons in a conversational tone. Considering his education and his mentor Justus Forward's views, he would have tried to teach about living morally in an unpredictable world beyond understanding.

He likely wore a wig and a robe of black wool or silk. Two strips of white cloth, known as Geneva bands or pastoral tabs, would have hung from the front of his collar. His handwritten sermons may have been like Reverend Justus Forward's written sermons: tiny booklets that looked exactly like their journals. Sometimes Rufus used brief notes. When he spoke without notes, at least in the early 1770s, he found it unusual enough to mention in his journal, as when he "extemporized the whole not having a Word writ."

Pastors routinely exchanged pulpits with one another, such as a three-way exchange in 1771 when Rufus "preach'd at Suffield, Mr. Gay [Suffield] at

The Journals of Rufus Hawley, Avon, Connecticut

North-Windsor, & Mr Hinsdale [North Windsor] at Northington." In 1798, he exchanged pulpits with at least fifteen other parishes, and seven pastors preached in his parish. This level of cooperation required planning and the support of the colony-wide General Association of Connecticut (established in 1709).

The Hartford North Association, mentioned earlier, was part of the General Association of Connecticut ministers, made up at this time of eight district associations. Ministers in Hartford North—from the towns and parishes of Farmington, Hartford, Simsbury and Windsor—met monthly in meetinghouses and ministers' homes for support, fellowship and study; at their meetings, they also settled parish disputes and certified candidates for the ministry. At a typical Hartford North Association meeting, which lasted two days, the members planned, prayed and discussed religion. Their friendships strengthened as they shared books and notes and heard one another preach sermons. Rufus also recorded hearing sermons by ministers visiting from New Jersey, Vermont and Philadelphia. The public also was invited to listen to the sermon portion of the meetings.

The General Association and its district associations were part of a Connecticut pastor's strong communication network, and pastors helped shape public opinion. During the American Revolution, British sympathizers described the clergy as the Black Regiment—influential and patriotic leaders in black robes. Pastors were well-informed by their encounters with visitors and travelers, and they had messengers to help spread the word of news and needs. They shared letters and publications and read the *Connecticut Courant* (established 1764) and the *Connecticut Evangelical Magazine* (1800–15), edited by many of Rufus's friends.

Almost one year after his ordination, Rufus Hawley married Deborah Kent. His 1770 journal is missing, but the September 25 wedding ceremony is in Northington's vital records as the marriage of "Rev. Rufus Hawley of Northington" and "Deborah Kent of Suffield." The marriage also appears in the vital records of both Farmington and Suffield.

Before Reverend Cotton Mather married in 1703, he hoped that his fiancée, Elizabeth, would be a good example as a wife, mother and neighbor and that she would read suitable books and improve herself by taking notes on the sermons. Rufus did not write of Deborah's qualifications, but they knew each other well and seemed to have patiently chosen each other with delight.

In addition to her duties as a mother, Deborah Hawley would visit around the region, entertain visitors in her home, raise and preserve food, make cheese, cook and do chores in the house and garden and on the farm. A few brief clues in the journals indicate that Deborah also had excellent sewing skills, for she made quilts and clothing and may have taught fine needlework. Her husband rarely wrote about her in the journals, but when he did so, it was always with respect.

1771

MAY 30 Thursday fair & moderate. being wak'd out of sleep a little before twelve oclock last night, I got up & married David Bristoll & Lois Hart, & Daniel Woodford & Ruth Thomson before one this Morning. Spent the Day at my Frame & Studying

AUGUST 4 DD fair & extream hot. preach a.m. an old sermon, & p.m. from Eccle. 9.12. and baptized Timothy Ruggles, Son to the Revd Rufus and Mrs Deborah Hawley.

Newly married, Rufus Hawley, thirty, began to build a house. In February 1770, right after his ordination, he had purchased three and a quarter acres from William Ford, located east of the Farmington River and near the meetinghouse. He spent spring days with friends "gitting timber for my House" and began framing in May. Three weeks later, he wrote that "this Day I had my House rais'd. Spent ye Day on ye Bu[siness]." Construction continued for almost a year, with a joiner, two apprentices and the pastor working into the fall.

Deborah Hawley's church in Suffield formally recommended her to "ye Chh in Northington" so she could join her husband's church. Then, on a stormy and rainy June 29, Rufus and Deborah's first child was born. They named the blue-eyed boy Timothy Ruggles, after Rufus's father, Timothy, and for Deborah's grandfather Benjamin Ruggles. "This day we had a Son born about a quarter before 10 o'clock in the forenoon: spent the Day waiting upon Mrs Hawley."

The tired father "preach'd old sermons" that Sunday, and on Monday he "took care of Mrs. Hawley our Nurse being busy washing." Helpful sisters arrived on Tuesday: Abigail Hawley, Ruth Kent and Lucy Kent Phelps. Four days after Timothy's birth, Rufus needed milk and "rode over the [Farmington] River after cow." On a hot Sunday, August 4, Rufus wrote in his journal that he "baptized Timothy Ruggles, Son to the Revd Rufus Hawley & Mrs Deborah Hawly."

With a new baby and constant visitors, Deborah, an affectionate mother, welcomed the assistance of Rufus's sister Deborah, who came for two extended visits. His sister Abigail stayed for a month to spin, Caroline Woodbridge of South Hadley stayed for five weeks and Hannah Blanchard moved in that December. Deborah's niece Andrea Fowler came in 1773 and stayed for over a year.

Rufus had a new parish, a new wife, a new house, a new farm and a new baby. This year, he made a bread chest and soap, planted an apple orchard and tended crops. He hoed the garden, which over the course of the journals had corn, beans, carrots, beets, cabbage, turnips, Indian corn, pumpkins, oats, rye and wheat. In his barnyard were oxen, cows, horses, sheep, turkeys and pigs to house, feed, water, chase and sometimes slaughter. His hay fields provided food for the some of the animals in the winter. Rufus made "a Hovel for my creatures at my House" with help from Ensign Cornelius Thomson. He built and rebuilt fences, writing when his sons were older that he "Help'd the boys rectify Fence a little." He plowed with sure-footed oxen on stony fields, burned fallow fields, got his shoes mended and his horse shod, had his grain ground into flour at the gristmill and helped saw logs at the sawmill.

A typical Northington farm at this time belonged to Thomas Gleason. The inventory at his death this year listed twenty sheep, a mare, a colt, a cow and a heifer. When Rufus came to the house to pay his respects, as he undoubtedly did, he would have found the house furnished with some fine things: a valuable "great chest," a table and a book collection.

Pastoral duties occupied Rufus Hawley's days and nights. "Being wak'd out of sleep a little before twelve oclock last night, I got up & married David Bristoll and Lois Hart, & Daniel Woodford & Ruth Thomson, before one o'clock this morning." Mary Bird Woodford was born four months later. In another wedding ceremony on a rainy November evening, Rufus married Abel Dago, "a Negro," and Lucy Way, "a squaw." After Phinehas Rowlenson Ford, age two, son to Thomas and Hannah Ford, died of a scald, Rufus preached the next Sunday "mostly extemporaneously." Human life, he said, was like new morning grass that could dry and wither by evening.

Following the example of Reverend Justus Forward, Rufus helped teach young men on their way to the ministry. He helped examine and grant his Turkey Hills cousin Abel Forward (Yale, 1768) a license to preach, and on an autumn Sunday, he admitted the nineteen-year-old son of Northington's late pastor, Aaron Jordan Booge (Yale, 1774), to church membership.

This summer, ministers from the Hartford North Association came to Northington when Rufus hosted his first Circular Lecture, a milestone for him. It was also a good day for Deborah, strong enough to hear a sermon in the meetinghouse, her first time there since Timothy's birth. The baby seemed to be thriving, for the journals say the doctor came only once, and after taking medicine "the child got better." Rufus's mother, Rachel—rarely mentioned in the journal—came for the weekend and saw her grandson's baptism.

The biggest local news was the grand new meetinghouse under construction in Farmington, with a large sanctuary, high ceilings, a delicately carved high pulpit and a soaring spire. Rufus saw the marvelous sight one hot July day, riding "to Town again to see them raise their Meeting-House." The national news was the revolution forming in the American minds and hearts; Rufus prayed with the militia company at morning and night during October's training day, when Northington's militia company practiced for emergencies and military action.

On New Year's Eve, Rufus and Deborah's house was still under construction, and baby Timothy was well:

> *Thanks be to God for his unspeakable*
> *gift of wha*[t?] *has purchased the*
> *comforts of life & eternal*
> *glory for unworthy Man.*

1772

JULY 8 Wednesday fair & very hot. I mov'd with my Family into my own House.

SEPTEMBER 9 Wednesday fair & hot till Evening then there was a shower. This Day was comminsment at New-Haven & I took my Second Degree. The Performances were very entertaining.

Storms in March and April that "snow'd & blow'd" left snow three feet deep. Running out of hay for his animals by mid-April, Rufus turned to his neighbors, who gave him some of their supplies. Visitors in sleighs kept coming by, and one January day, Rufus barely kept track of the crowd. His sisters Abigail and Deborah from Turkey Hills "call'd at our Dwelling," and Abigail stayed for weeks. Rufus's uncle Abel Forward stopped in with his daughter Sabrina, along with his cousin Elijah Hawley and his wife, from Farmington. Perfect strangers visited, along with "another Slay load of People that we don't know who they were."

In May, news came of the death of Temperance Clap Pitkin, forty, the wife of Farmington pastor Reverend Timothy Pitkin. On the frosty morning following her death, Rufus "went to the Funeral of Mrs Pitkin Mrs Hawley went with me; I was one of the Bariers [pall bearers]." Mrs. Pitkin did not live to see the completion of her husband's grand meetinghouse, an event that Rufus attended on November 15. At year's end, Rufus "rode to Town to the Dedication of the new Meeting House."

There were barn raisings at the homes of Samuel Thompson and weaver Thomas Gleason. Construction continued on the Hawleys' house with help from cousin Abel Hawley, a joiner, and it took two weeks to finish the chimney. Two Sundays in a row, Rufus "preach'd old Sermons being so taken up by Masons & Joyners I had no time to Study."

On a fair and hot July day, the pastor "assisted about laying a Harth in my Kitchin." Construction had taken thirteen months. With Timothy probably beginning to walk, Rufus wrote on July 8, "I mov'd with my Family into my own House." Tragedy almost struck when someone got careless with the broom that swept hot coals from the bake oven. "Our House catch'd on

Reverend Rufus Hawley's journal, July 13, 1772: "Monday fair & hot. did chores & catechis'd the children. our house catch'd on fire by Reason of throwing an oven Broom out at the Door; but by a kind Providence we Soon put it out." *Hawley-August Collection, Avon Free Public Library. Photograph by John Pecora.*

fire by Reason of throwing an oven Broom out at the Door, but by a kind Providence we Soon put it out." The Hawleys would live in this house for eighteen years.

After Rufus rode "out to invite Some Hands to give me a Spell" in August, twenty-three helpers arrived at the farm the next day. "People," he wrote, "gave me a spell clearing away the Lumber from my House & gitting the Dirt from the back Side of the house to the foreside." Two strong young men helped build fences when Rufus "assisted Elijah & Charles Woodford who were Setting up a fence for me."

Ministers also depended on one another to help, and at a moment's notice. That quick knock on the door or that frantic call across the field might be a neighbor or messenger bringing urgent news. When Farmington pastor Timothy Pitkin attended the July funeral of Wethersfield pastor James Lockwood, Rufus stepped in to assist in Farmington. "Mrs. Hawley & I went to Town to the Wedding of James Root & Mercy Stedman whom I married, Mr. Pitkin being gone to the Funeral of Mr Lockwood of Weathersfield who departed this Life yesterday."

There were many times in his pastorate when Rufus had to act fast, and a gesture such as substituting on short notice for a colleague would likely earn him a favor. In 1774, he wrote that "Mr Bissel lately had his Shoulder & Collar Bone put out, & being unable to preach, I preach'd for him, and Mr [Aaron] Booge for me." In 1783, he "preach'd at New-cambridge, Mr [Samuel] Newell having Some Time past been Siez'd with the num Palsy, & incapacitated to preach." In 1781, he substituted for Reverend Samuel Stebbins of Simsbury and "baptized Hepzibah, Daughter to Amazia Humphrey; which I did at his House, the Child being dangerously Sick, & Mr. Stebbins being unwell, & not able to go out to do it." After Reverend Jonathan Marsh of New Hartford died in 1794, Rufus volunteered to fill in with no expectation of receiving reciprocal help: "preach'd at New-hartford by way of Gift Mr Marsh being dead."

Although Rufus willingly helped others in need, he sometimes did not have the assistance or the people in the pews that he needed. At a May church meeting to assign tasks, Deacon Ebenezer Miller agreed to provide the bread and wine for communion, but with "few Brethren at Meeting," no other jobs were assigned. On a bleak and rainy Sunday this February, it was "very difficult going to Meeting and there was but three Persons came in the forenoon & I did not preach but in the afternoon I preach'd fr there was more." On a cold and snowy Sunday in 1774, he preached in the morning but it was "so tedious & there were so few at Meeting that I dismis'd the Meeting at Noon."

The Journals of Rufus Hawley, Avon, Connecticut

An empty meetinghouse could be due to something more than disinterest or wretched weather. Soon after these tedious Sundays, Rufus was "taken sick" on February 19. Dr. Timothy Hooker of Farmington came to see him, and over the next week he "went to Bed & sweat," "kept to my bed cheif of the Day," "took a vomit" and had "a Sick Day & very Sick Night." Dr. Hooker & Dr. Hosmer, he wrote, "visited me every Day since I was sick." After nine miserable days he was "so much better that I just walk'd abroad this Day & read & rote considerable."

The sickness was a killer. That Monday, March 9, Rufus "visited the sick all Day till 9 at Night." On Tuesday, Medad and Phebe Hart lost their daughter Charity, age seven, and the next day he "made a Prayer" at her funeral at Reuben Miller's house. Three days later, he visited and prayed with Sarah Fowler Miller, who died the next day after delivering a stillborn son. "They were lay'd out together, & both put onto one coffin." Two days after that, the exhausted pastor visited the deceased woman's gravely ill mother-in-law, Sarah Allan Miller. Rufus did chores, but as for studying, he managed to do "but a little."

Before daybreak the next day, Sunday, Rufus was summoned again "to go to Capt [Jonathan] Miller's they supposing his Wife was a dying." That was correct, as it turned out; the funeral for grandmother Sarah Allan Miller; her daughter-in-law, Sarah Fowler Miller; and the infant was on a snowy Monday at Captain Jonathan Miller's home. Rufus "attended the Funerals of Capt Millers Wife, Elisha Millers Wife & Infant Babe: Elisha's Wife & Child were carried to the Captns where Prayers were made for all the Mourners; then the dead were all carried to ye grave together, & all buried in one grave." Finally, the pastor's emotions spilled out. What he saw at Cider Brook cemetery "was such a scene as I never beheld before."

The Miller tragedy, less than three years into Rufus's pastorate, may have boosted people's confidence in their new pastor, and his wife. Appreciated and well-liked, Deborah Hawley was a kind neighbor and expert needleworker. When their critically ill friend Reverend Gideon Mills, pastor of West Simsbury (today Canton), took a turn for the worse, they hastily rode on August 4 to his home. He "di'd a little before we got there," and Deborah stayed on to make "mourning Dress for ye family."

The journal this year has the entry showing that Deborah also taught needlework. "Mr Charles Granger of Suffield," Rufus wrote on May 28, "came to our Dwelling & brought Rhoda Hanchet his Wives Daughter who came to learn the Tayleresess Trade of my Wife." Deborah's work fits a pattern found by historians in families of Yale-educated ministers at this time: they were often talented needleworkers and style-setters for their communities. It is possible that along with tailoring, Deborah taught decorative needlework for bed hangings, pictures, clothing, pocketbooks and more.

At the Yale commencement this year, Rufus Hawley wrote that, with his sister Abigail in the audience, he received what he called his "Second Degree," his master of arts. The journal had not indicated that he was to receive this advanced degree, and that day he simply wrote that "the performances were very entertaining." His MA degree was probably one of those that Yale awarded automatically three years after graduation, if the man had a record of good conduct.

At year's end, a routine event brought the word "Christmas" into the journal for the only time, and in a way that suggested Rufus's curiosity about the celebration. Puritans and their descendants treated Christmas as a routine day, nothing like the custom in England of drunken revelers and begging. The circumstances that led up to Rufus's encounter with Christmas in an Episcopal church started when he married Reverend Dan Foster, twenty-four, and Rebecca Booge, eighteen, in Northington on December 22. It was "a good wedding," and guests at the ceremony included Reverend Timothy Pitkin (Farmington) and Reverend Theodore Hinsdale (North Windsor). Rufus killed a hog that morning, so perhaps there was fresh meat at the celebration. The following day, Rufus and others rode to Windsor "to wait upon Mr Foster & his Lady home." Returning to Northington on Christmas Day 1772, Rufus deliberately stopped at St. Andrew's Episcopal Church in Scotland parish (today Bloomfield). "Stopped at Scotland to see the Church People perform their Christmas service: Then we rode to Amasa Case's & Sup'd, & then home."

On December 31, Rufus was at Sarah Bishop's bedside when a surgeon removed fluid from her body. "Went to see the opperation of Tapping perform'd on Sergt Bishops Wife." That night, he seemed to be at a loss for words.

1773: NO JOURNAL

On April 27, Deborah gave birth to their second son, Rufus Forward Hawley, and his father baptized the baby with light blue eyes on May 30. Baptism was open only to the children of a married couple, and the pastor carefully kept track of every child's status. He wrote the word "illegitimate" in the parish vital records to record the birth of Medad and Anne Woodruff's son, a baby born ten months before their 1775 marriage. It was not until twenty-four years later that the Woodruffs brought their nine children to Rufus for baptism; his sermon that Sunday in 1799 spoke on the importance of a good conscience and of baptism's saving power.

A good number of babies did arrive less than nine months after a wedding. The vital records of Northington indicate that at this time, about one-third of the parish's brides were pregnant when they married. Lucy Darrin Booge, the daughter-in-law of the parish's first pastor, had been one of these new brides, delivering her son three months after her 1778 wedding to Oliver Booge.

In late December, Massachusetts citizens dressed as Mohawk Indians dumped the tea cargo from the British ship *Dartmouth* into Boston Harbor. Refusing to pay the British duty on tea, they left the 342 casks bobbing in the frigid water.

1774

OCTOBER 27 *Thursday fair & very warm for the Season our People had a Training, Pray'd with the Company: Sergt Joseph Millar made a dinner for the Company, & invited Mrs Hawley & I to dine with him; we went.*

DECEMBER 7 *Wednesday Cloudy & rain'd Some. This Day about Sun Set, we had a third Son born; I spent the Day upon the Business.*

Rufus taught at the Cider Brook schoolhouse this spring, a relatively safe place for children. A more hazardous place, as noted by accidents in his journals, was a child's home. In January, Timothy Foot, age two, the illegitimate son of twenty-year-old Hannah Woodford, was scalded at his house. Rufus went to see the toddler immediately and was called back at midnight. Timothy died five days later. Unwilling to perform an illegitimate child's funeral or preside at his burial, Rufus still tried to comfort the family. Before going with Deborah and their sons, Timothy and little Rufus (called Rufus Forward by his father), to Suffield, he stopped their sleigh at "widow Woodfords," where he "pray'd with them on Account of the Death of the above mentioned Child, previous to its Burial."

During the spring, it seems that plans were underway for having his parents move from their Turkey Hills farm (the move occurred two years later in 1776). At this time, however, the idea was for Samuel Booge and Timothy Hawley to swap farms. When that plan fell through, wrote Rufus, Peter Buel Gleason "agreed to take Fathers farm upon Shars [shares] this summer." At year's end, Peter Gleason would marry Timothy's daughter (Rufus's sister), Deborah.

Rufus's work on his own house and barn continued. After digging a deep well, he shifted the dirt to the front of the house; he took a week to frame and raise his new barn and hammered shingles on its roof. At the sawmill, he got boards and "boarded the Great Doors of my Barn." Cold weather that had "not been known in the present Age at this Season of the year" hindered May planting. Water froze an inch thick in tubs, and farmers tried plowing on ground frozen so hard that "it would bear a Grown Person to walk upon it & not give way." A frost on June 1 killed Indian corn and other crops.

Northington's unease over the looming hostilities with England was growing, and Rufus's sermon on a spring Sunday urged the people to find peace by having faith. At the Sons of Liberty parade in Farmington at 6:00 p.m. on May 19, before England's blockade of Boston, the Hawleys might have been among the almost one thousand people who went to a forty-five-foot pole, perhaps topped with a flag, to voice their protests and agree on revolutionary resolutions.

Northington men were training to fight. In early October, Rufus wrote that "our People had a Training, the Officers desir'd me to pray with the Company, which I did." Afterward, he dined with Ensign Joseph Woodford and the company. Three weeks later, he prayed with the people at another training, dining that night with Deborah and Sergeant Joseph Miller's militia company. In November, all of Connecticut's militia companies mustered to inspect arms and determine battle readiness.

At September's Yale commencement, Aaron Jordan Booge, age twenty-two, was in the senior class of thirty students. Rufus had helped train Aaron, and the young man was the son of Northington's first pastor. At the General Association meeting in New Haven soon after, Rufus and his colleagues examined Aaron and other ministry candidates. Rufus wrote that a "Mr Fisk's moral character being not very good, he was put by." Faring better than Mr. Fisk, Aaron Booge received his license for the ministry, and the cycle of education began again. Aaron's brother Publius Virgilius Booge, age eight—called Virgil by Rufus—"began to study with me, & recited his first lesson."

In order to expand his four-acre farm this fall, Rufus purchased twelve acres "in the common field in the old Farm," a term widely used today with Avon Old Farms School, Old Farms Road, Avon Old Farms Inn and Avon Old Farms Hotel. Also busy with family matters, he admitted his sister Abigail Hawley to full communion in the Northington church, and on November 9, he performed his sister Deborah's wedding to Peter Buel Gleason of Northington.

At sunset on a cloudy and rainy December 7, Rufus and Deborah's third son, Jesse Dudley Hawley, was born. All was well with Jesse, but a Simsbury family was facing a crisis with their baby. When Colonel Jonathan Humphrey came to Rufus's house desperate to save his granddaughter's soul, the pastor went immediately to Simsbury, where the colonel's granddaughter, Lodanne Pinney, lay "dangerously sick" and unbaptized. The problem about baptizing her, Rufus said, was that her parents had not "renewed their Covenant" and were not church members. The helpful pastor, however, used the Halfway Covenant and baptized Lodanne on the basis of her grandfather's membership in the Simsbury church. "[I] went & baptiz'd it, which I did on the Colonel's Right."

Rufus's night ride to the Pinneys' house in Simsbury had been "fair & remarcable pleasant," and it was not much farther to ride on to his father's house in Turkey Hills. There, he picked up little Rufus, almost two years old, who had been with his grandparents for over a month. Perhaps Deborah wanted to have the inquisitive toddler out from underfoot during Jesse's birth, safe from hazardous fireplaces and hot liquids.

The year ended with huge snowdrifts, Aaron Booge's preaching in Northington and Deborah's recuperation from Jesse's birth. Timothy, little Rufus and the baby all needed attention, and their father sounded tired, writing on December 28 that it was "very windy & cold, & Snow'd extream hard all day. I tended Cattle, cut Wood, & made Fires, & that was eno' work for the Day."

In the past five years, Rufus Hawley had become a settled pastor, married Deborah, built a house and a farm and had three sons. He knew it could all be taken away in an instant. This year, an unsettling and almost permanent measure of year-end gloom crept into his closing lines on New Year's Eve:

Adieu to the year, for another got here—
Time flies, & Man dies

1775: No Journal

The year 1775 begins a span of eight years during the American Revolution where only two journals survive (1778 and 1781). As it is unlikely that Rufus stopped writing, perhaps the historic significance of these journals led to their separation from the collection.

Jesse Dudley Hawley's baptism on January 15 began a year of worry and dread. After the battles of Lexington and Concord in April, Connecticut called up six hundred militiamen to defend Massachusetts. Farmington's Sixth Company of ninety-four men and four officers left for Boston in May. Farmers picked up their guns and tried to follow orders. Samuel Gleason of Northington wrote in his diary on August 15 that "a man was flogged ten stripes for saucy talk to officers." The Connecticut General Assembly urged ministers to preach about unity and to pray for the country's leaders and liberties.

Preoccupied with funerals this year, Rufus recorded twice as many Northington deaths as usual. But there was new life, too, with Truman Ford's birth on July 4 and his baptism by Rufus a month later. Truman, it turned out, would break his pastor's heart.

6

TREAT ME AS SHE OUGHT

Revolutionary Times, 1776–1783

1776: NO JOURNAL

At their annual meeting in June, the General Association of ministers approved sending a letter to Connecticut's pastors that blamed the people's immorality and misbehavior for England's tyranny. The association asked ministers, professors, parents and children to unite "with penitent Hearts, to confess and deplore their Sins."

There was more to cause concern than this letter from the association, for families were reeling from farewells and losses. Colonel Noadiah Hooker had recruited a company of forty-five men from Farmington and its six parishes. Rufus soon recorded in the vital records the loss of five Northington recruits: Joseph Bishop, thirty-three, died at Fort Ann, New York; Asaph Fuller, sixteen, and David Fuller died in the "army at New York"; and Imri Judd, sixteen, and Nathaniel Bunnell, died of scarlet fever in the "Northern Army." Adding to these grievous losses was a dysentery epidemic, with its victims probably counted among Northington's thirty-six deaths during 1776 and 1777, a figure more than three times higher than the annual deaths in the following two years.

Rufus surely found a measure of happiness at the two-day ordination of Reverend Aaron Jordan Booge, age twenty-four. He had helped educate Aaron, attended his 1774 Yale graduation and seen Turkey Hills struggle without a settled pastor. The ordination council of eleven ministers gathered at John and Martha Thrall's house in November to question the candidate and examine his credentials. At the ceremony the next morning, Rufus described "the solemn setting apart [of the] said Mr. Booge [to] the sacred work of the Christian ministry and pastoral office in this place." In one of his first official acts, Reverend Booge released Rufus's parents, Timothy and Rachel Hawley, from their membership in the Turkey Hills church and "recommended [them] to the chh of Christ in Northington."

At 3:00 a.m. on Christmas morning, General George Washington's twenty-four hundred troops rowed across the icy Delaware River toward fourteen hundred sleeping Hessian soldiers at Trenton. After devastating losses this first year of the American Revolution, Washington's crossing of the Delaware and his New Jersey victory would be jubilant news.

1777: NO JOURNAL

Rufus and Deborah's fourth son, George Washington Hawley, was born on January 26, and his father baptized Washington five weeks later. The four Hawley boys were safe for now, but the American Revolution continued its decimation of other Northington families. After Joseph Hart III, age seventeen, was shot by a British regular in late 1776 at King's Bridge in New York, his father, Joseph Hart Jr., had hastened to Stamford, Connecticut, to take care of his son. Young Joseph died there, and on the journey home to Northington, his grieving father died from pleurisy in New Haven.

Two hundred miles from Northington, the Continental army set up winter camp in Pennsylvania, at a place of which Northington would surely hear: Valley Forge.

1778

SEPTEMBER 16 Wednesday fair & moderate. This Day we had a fifth Son born about Sun Seting. Did Errands, Chors, &c.

NOVEMBER 20, Friday cheifly cloudy & cold, Snow'd a Small matter. The 2ᵈ Devision of Hessian Troops pass'd by Capt Forwards about 10 OClock: Mr. Forward & I Set out & Soon overtook them, & had considerable Conversation with some of their officers; parted with them on the west side of the Mountain, rode to Uncle Abel Forward's then to Brothers' & from there he rode for Southwick & home. Genl Poor's Brigade of American Troops were in Simsbury when I came along, (having this Day mov'd from the East Side of the Mountain over against my House, where they, together with Genl Maxwell & Genl Patterson's Brigades, have of late been encamp'd;) they are going to guard Genl Burgoin's Army to Some of the Southern States.

In the third year of the American Revolution, Northington residents gathered at the meetinghouse for a Continental Fast on April 22. Perhaps acting on that 1776 General Association letter about piety having a role in victory, Rufus preached on improving one's behavior. Word came early in the year that Northington's Zebulon Woodruff Jr. had died in New York, a soldier recorded in the vital records as "a prisoner among the enemy."

In the midst of war, Rufus's work still followed the rhythms of parish life. He taught school as a substitute for an ill Levi Thomson, carried grain to the mill for grinding, went to Benjamin Andrus to get his gun stocked and took a day to get his mare shod. He prayed with a woman visiting from Branford who fell from her carriage, writing that she was "flung out of a Shays and hurt." The pastor was hospitable when candidates for the ministry stopped by, and he married Lucy Darrin and Oliver Booge.

There were daily worries on the farm. When several of his sheep and cows went missing, Rufus searched for many weeks until finding his heifer in Wintonbury (today Bloomfield). The twenty cords of free wood the pastor received annually proved inadequate to keep the house heated. Too cold to work in his study on four Saturdays, he came to the pulpit each time with an "old sermon." The Hawleys now had four children and frequent visitors, but their annual allotment of free wood remained at a steady twenty cords.

Obtaining enough yarn was also a concern. Rufus spent five days in June riding his horse through the parish, "inviting the young women to give us a Spell of Spinning." Making clothes for four boys under age seven, the pregnant Deborah Hawley appreciated receiving wool and flax already spun into skeins and ready for weaving and knitting. About a week after Rufus's ride, the women gathered at the Hawleys' on a hot Monday for a party. "Towards 40 young Ladies who had been giving us a Spinning Spell, came to bring in their yarn & make us a Visit; They Sup'd with us: we had towards 60 Run Spun."

Late that summer, Rufus rode fifty miles to western Massachusetts on a four-day errand for his sister Deborah's husband, Peter Buel Gleason of Northington. Riding to Tyringham, Rufus met up with his brother-in-law Reverend Adonijah Bidwell, and the two traveled to Stockbridge to take a urine sample, which Rufus called "Brother Gleasons water." A Doctor Adams examined it for its smell, appearance and even taste. This ominous entry in the journal indicated diabetes or dropsy, conditions that would have caused urination changes, water retention, swollen tissues and possibly sudden heart failure. Rufus rode the forty miles home in one day, perhaps bearing dreaded news, and two years later Peter Buel Gleason died.

As the sun set on a "fair and moderate" September 16, Deborah Hawley gave birth to Orestes Kent Hawley. His father baptized the gray-eyed baby seven weeks later, writing on a cloudy Sunday, October 25, that he "baptiz'd Orestes Kent Son to the Rev Rufus Hawley." The Hawleys now had five boys, and help for Deborah soon arrived when her niece Maria Kent, age eighteen, came for a visit.

Maria's visit is important because it led to a passage in the journal that puts her and Uncle Rufus squarely in the middle of the American army and its British prisoners. When Rufus took Maria home to Suffield on Wednesday, November 18, 1778, "The 3rd & last Devision of British prisoners, taken with Gen'l Burgoin [British General John Burgoyne], were at Simsbury as we went along." The size of the crowd, it seemed, caused Rufus and Justus Forward to miss meeting up on the roadway. "Mr. Forward of Belchers Town came to our House [in Northington] & lodg'd, whom we miss'd & pass'd by Somewhere in Simsbury."

The next day, a snowy November 19, Justus Forward wrote in his 1778 diary that he left Rufus's house and "went in Talcott Road to Hartford, saw some brigades of Continental troops on the mountain [?] and some of our men."

Rufus spent that day visiting around Suffield. Riding back to Northington, he again met up with the British prisoners outside Turkey Hills, writing that he "overtook the 1st Devision of Hessian troops taken with Genl Burgoin." He finally caught up with Justus in Turkey Hills, and they stayed the night at the home of Justus's mother, Mercy Forward.

On Friday, November 20, it "Snow'd a Small matter," and "the 2^{d} Devision of Hessian troops pas'd by Capt Forwards about 10 OClock: Mr. Forward & I Set out & Soon overtook them, & had considerable Conversation with Some of their officers; parted with them on the west Side of the Mountain." Justus returned home to Belchertown, and Rufus headed for Northington, where he came across Continental army soldiers on their way to Virginia. "Gen's Poor's [General Enoch Poor] Brigade of American Troops were in Simsbury when I came along, (having this Day mov'd from the East Side of the Mountain over against my House, where they, together with Genl Maxwell [General William Maxwell] & Genl Patterson's [General John Paterson] Brigades have of late been encamp'd); they are going to guard Genl Burgoin's Army to Some of the Southern States." It is unclear what Rufus meant by "against my House," but it seems to imply that the troops were camping near his house at what would today be the west end of the street called Reverknolls.

These generals kept British prisoners in line, and Rufus tried to keep Mary Woodford in line. While he did not elaborate, it seems that he had so angered Mary Woodford that she had stopped attending church. On August 17, Reverend Theodore Hinsdale (North Windsor) and a Northington deacon met at Rufus's house and decided that Mrs. Woodford must return to church and treat her pastor with respect. "The Wido Mary Woodford having taken an Affront at a Reproof and Exhortation I gave her Some Time past, & absented from my Ministry; at her Desire and mine, Mr. Hinsdale & Deacon Dorchester came to my House to Settle the matter. They Spent half the Day or more on the Business; and finally advis'd her to return & attend upon my Ministry: and treat me as She ought to treat a Gospel Minister." This is the only time that Rufus wrote about a woman who exasperated him, except for six years before this, when he wrote briefly of a Sunday service where he read aloud Rhoda Thompson's confession of "drinking, Sabbath breaking & Fornication."

Northington celebrated Continental Thanksgiving on December 30, a tradition started in 1777, when the Continental Congress proclaimed a national day of thanksgiving with no labor or recreation. Rufus's New Year's Eve line was hopeful:

> *The Wheels of Time rode o'er*
> *and pass the year away;*
> *O may I be of God a lover,*
> *And meet a brighter Day.*

1779: NO JOURNAL

During Rufus Hawley's tenth anniversary as Northington's settled pastor, he enlarged his farm by purchasing 128 acres on the opposite (west) side of the Farmington River. Living nearby were David Gleason Sr. and his wife, Abigail. Deborah Hawley lived close enough to easily attend the quilting bee at their home in November.

David Gleason, a Northington Society clerk and tax collector, was a good friend to the Hawleys. He was someone whom Rufus definitely would have wanted to keep close, for Gleason family members, along with Harts and Nortons, held tight control of the society. Members of these three families held the pivotal positions of society moderator and clerk for almost three quarters of the society's meetings from 1753 to 1818. For years, David Gleason swept the church once a month and regularly attended Sunday services. He always wrote in his *Day Book* which Bible verse "Mr. Hawley" preached, except for one Sunday: "Don't remember tex [text]."

David Gleason did remember that Sunday in September at the meetinghouse when his pastor collected money for the people of New Haven. Two months earlier, forty-eight British ships with twenty-six hundred men had attacked Rufus's college town. His friend and former tutor, Reverend Napthali Daggett, had helped defend New Haven and died several months later of his injuries from being stabbed with bayonets and beaten with gun barrels.

In war-weary Northington, there was vigorous pride at being part of the United States. One of David Gleason's journal entries this year noted the December 9 meetinghouse service for the "*United States Thanksgiving day.*" His upper-case cursive letters were striking, carefully written by a new American.

1780: No Journal

On May 19, a daytime darkness covered southern New England. The cause, unknown to Northington that terrifying day, was a massive wildfire in Canada and a cloud cover that blocked the sun. Midday was like midnight, with cattle returning to their barns, chickens roosting, birds ceasing to sing, bats flitting in the air and frogs peeping nighttime calls. The Connecticut legislature, meeting in Hartford, decided that if it was Judgment Day, they better spend it doing their duty and not adjourn. Poet John Greenleaf Whittier described the day in his "Tent on the Beach" (1867):

> *The low hung sky*
> *Was black with ominous clouds, save where its rim*
> *Was fringed with a dull glow, like that which climbs*
> *The crater's sides from the red hell below.*

Surely the people of Northington called on their pastor for an explanation and comfort.

In September, General George Washington came to Hartford to meet with Jean Baptiste, Comte de Rochambeau, the leader of the five-thousand-man French army that had recently arrived to aid the American cause. Five thousand people turned out in Hartford to see Washington and Rochambeau receive a thirteen-gun salute. Perhaps Rufus, Deborah and their sons, including George Washington, age three, were in the crowd. A little over a year later, Rochambeau's troops would fight alongside the Americans at the British defeat in Yorktown.

1781

APRIL 14 Saturday fair, windy & exceeding cold for the Season. This Morning, not far from one OClock, Mrs Hawley was deliv'd of a Male Child, which is our Sixth Son. I rode to Mr. Elihu Hookers & brought Miss Abi Hart to our House, then rode almost to Couzin Gad Hawley's to accompany Mrs Mix Homewards; after which I return'd & did Some Chores.

JUNE 22 fair & hot. call'd upon Mr Morgan. rode to Litchfield, din'd with Mr Champion, then rode to Harwington, call upon Mr Perry a little while, then rode home.

June 22 was hot as Rufus finished off a four-day visit through northwest Connecticut by dining in Litchfield with its pastor, Reverend Judah Champion (Yale, 1751). Their talk must have turned to the recent murder of five people in the nearby town of Washington. It had been a snowy night in 1780 at the farmhouse of Caleb Mallory, his wife and their three grandchildren. Barnett Davenport, age nineteen, the Mallorys' boarder and farmhand, killed the couple and one child as they slept and then set fire to the house with the two other children inside. It was Reverend Champion who likely transcribed Davenport's confession in Newgate Prison.

Rufus's thoughts at hearing this story may have turned to his own five young children and to the young man boarding in his own house. Dr. Solomon Everest, about twenty-one years old, appears in the journal from time to time but always as a trusted friend.

Deborah Hawley neared the birth of her sixth child, and friends and relations continually dropped by the house, including Justus Forward and a visitor from Vermont. For two days in April, Rufus made soap, an unusual chore for him to mention but one that must have been a help to Deborah. Then, on a windy and "exceeding cold" Saturday, April 14, blue-eyed Zerah Hawley was born at one o'clock in the morning. "Mrs. Hawley was deliv'd of a Male Child, which is our Sixth Son." The previous day, Rufus had ridden to the west side of the parish to fetch midwife Anna Mix. There is no mention of Doctor Everest, indicating a preference for the trusted midwife over the male doctor. Having babies may have seemed routine by now, for the journal entry about Zerah's birth did not receive that important pointing finger.

On the day of Zerah's birth, Rufus rode to Elihu Hooker's to fetch Miss Abi Hart, age nineteen. Young and unmarried, Abi had four younger brothers and sisters and knew how to care for children. That same endless day, Rufus took midwife Anna Mix back to her home. Having been up probably all night at Zerah's birth and then busy all day Saturday, Rufus was dutifully in the pulpit on Sunday. His strain shows by his failure to record in his journal the verse he preached. Exhausted with the hubbub at home, he neglected this usually meticulous journal entry. He was also terribly worried, for Deborah was "extremely ill" after the delivery. Rufus took care of her, and a week later, a Mrs. Nott came to help.

Abi Hart, Mrs. Nott and perhaps others helped Deborah and the children. In the coming weeks, Rufus kept busy "plowing my Garden," planting seeds, catechizing the children at the meetinghouse and baptizing a new baby almost every Sunday. He wrote in his journal that on a fair and warm Sunday, June 3, he "Baptized Zerah son to Rev'd Rufus Hawley, & Mrs Deborah his wife," entering the almost two-month-old Zerah into the parish baptism records as "son to Rev'd Rufus Hawley, & Deborah his Wife."

Four months later and with plenty of hands at home to look after the children, Deborah accompanied her husband to visit Lovelytown, the western part of Northington. She was soon able to go on a fifty-mile journey with her nursing baby to Tyringham, Massachusetts, and spend ten days with her sister Ruth Kent Bidwell and brother-in-law Reverend Adonijah Bidwell.

Rufus continued to work on plans for a new house on the west bank of the Farmington River, located almost directly across from his present home and meetinghouse. In May, he helped Mr. Solomon Whitman and "Some other Men who were running the Line round my Land over the River & in the Meadow."

Great excitement was also unfolding in Farmington, and Rufus did not want to miss a thing. Rochambeau was bringing his French army of over five thousand men (divided into four divisions) from Newport, Rhode Island, to join the Continental army outside New York City, at what is today White Plains. His route led from Hartford, through West Hartford and straight through Farmington. The first unit of French soldiers arrived in Farmington on June 25, 1781, and camped along Main Street, one and a half miles south from what is today the intersection of Routes 4 and 10. Two days of rain that Rufus described as plentiful and brisk delayed the army's departure, and he was able to visit the muddy scene. After writing and chores, he "rode to Town p.m. to See Some French Troops which were encamp'd there being on their way to Join Genl Washington on the North River." David Gleason wrote in his own journal of seeing the French in Farmington "moving to the North River."

At Yale in September, Rufus observed with clear delight that commencement was "a publick one this year, which there has not been this seven years before" because of the war. He then returned home, just in time to baptize the "dangerously sick" Lucy Brockway, the infant daughter of non–church members Joseph Brockway Jr. and his wife, Lucy. Using the Halfway Covenant, he baptized baby Lucy on the "Right of Mr. Philip Lilly's wives Right, the Parents not having renew'd their Covt." The pastor's comforting gesture, Mrs. Lilly's cooperation or Lucy's death may have prompted the Brockways to join the church, for two months later he admitted them to full communion, baptizing them and their children, Anna and Hosea.

That same Sunday, November 11, Rufus wrote that he "baptized Lone Girl which is given to Sergt Elnn Hart, by Eunice Hart." This unusual journal entry highlights a baptism that was not listed in the Northington vital records: Eunice Hart gave her daughter to her brother Elnathan and his wife, Ruth. The Harts had only two children, Linus nineteen, and Obedience, twelve, so perhaps they were glad to take in Eunice's child, a girl who could one day help with housework and who seemed so alone.

Rufus wrote often of comforting people, of baptizing critically ill babies and of offering prayers of hope. When cousin Samuel Bird visited with his handicapped wife, Rhoda Hawley Bird, in February, Rufus recorded that "Couzin Samll Bird came to our House, & brought his wife upon a Bed in a Slay. She is not able to go a step, nor hant been for Some years." And then there were the times when the pastor took to the woods in a frantic search for a lost child, kept vigil or tried to heal a child's wounds.

Childhood dangers lurked in the kitchen, the farmyard, the woods and the river. On a hot afternoon in June, Rufus rushed to help find a boy. "Looked after a Boy of Leiut Isaiah Thomson's that was Sepos'd to be lost in the woods. The boy was found afterwards drowned in the River." Possibly the child was unfamiliar with the woods, unaccustomed to the perils of the Farmington River and tempted by a cool dip on a hot spring afternoon.

Several months after this, another child needed help. Monday, December 3, was clear, with temperatures warm enough for children to be outdoors, warm enough to melt that morning's fresh snow. There were five sons at the farmhouse of Ensign William and Catherine Ford: William, age nine; Giles, eight; Truman, six; Judah, almost four; and Chancy, sixteen months old.

Just after sunset, Truman fell into a well that his father had been digging and, wrote Rufus, "stop'd up about a quarter of the way: He broke his thigh, & fractur'd his Skull very much." A desperate call went out in the dark for the pastor. "Being sent for, I went & pray'd with him," and during that long night, Rufus stayed nearby. Truman "had his Thigh Set between Midnight and Day, which I assisted in doing." A few hours later, on Tuesday, the surgeon took a small saw to cut a hole into Truman's skull. "His Head was trepan'd about Noon and fourteen or 15 Pecies of bone of the Skull Bone taken out."

On Wednesday, during a snowstorm, Rufus was home "quite ill" with a cold, but on Friday, four days after the accident, he returned to Truman's house and "assisted about dressing Truman Ford's wounds. The Helm of the Brain is broke, near a tea Spoon-full of his Brains came out."

With neither time nor fortitude to write a new sermon, Rufus preached an old one that Sunday. The Fords may have blamed themselves for the accident, for their pastor preached extemporaneously that afternoon about the blameless and upright man Job, who also had lost family members. He went back to the house seven times during the next two weeks to help Truman. During these long hours, he "pray'd with Truman Ford," "assisted about dressing Truman's Head," "assisted in dressing Truman's Head & Thigh a.m." and "help'd dress Trumans Head &c." On December 24, just before the boy died, he "help'd dress Truman" for the last time.

On Christmas Day, Rufus "attended the funeral of Truman Ford" and "pray'd on the Occation." The following Sunday morning, he preached from the book of Acts 20:9 about a young man raised from the dead. Worn out, he preached an old sermon that afternoon. On New Year's Eve, a week after Truman Ford's death, there was nothing left to say: "Adieu to 1781."

1782: NO JOURNAL

After six boys in eleven years, a baby girl joined the Hawley family on November 18, sister to Timothy, eleven; Rufus, nine; Jesse, seven; Washington, five; Orestes, four; and Zerah, one. Her name, Sophia, meant wisdom. The Hawley family was complete with seven children, about average for an eighteenth-century Connecticut family. It was the end of babies for Deborah and the end of the American Revolution. That fall, marching north after their victory in Yorktown in the fall of 1781, the French troops passed through Farmington for the last time.

1783

JANUARY 5 Sunday DD Cloudy & Snowd considerable in the Morning moderate. Preach'd from Mat.17.5 a.m. admitted Doctr Solomon Everest & Amelia his wife into full Communion, & administered the Sacrament. preach'd p.m. & baptiz'd Sophia Daughter to the Rev'd Rufus Hawley & Mrs Deborah his wife.

OCTOBER 29 Wednesday foggy & misty, we all rode to Mr Gailord's Parish, & attended a Fast there. Mr Stebbins & I preach'd. the Design of the Fasts was principally to implore the outpouring of the Spirit. we lodg'd at Capt Williams's, Mr Gailords Quarters.

Rufus was at the top of his game in 1783 and would be for some time, with his congregation searching more desperately for spiritual growth. Perhaps this was the year to freeze in time. His seven children were well, his parents lived nearby, his farm had been operating for twelve years and he was strong enough to sail across a flooded valley. On a snowy Sunday afternoon, January 5, he "baptiz'd Sophia Daughter to the Rev'd Rufus Hawley & Mrs Deborah his wife."

A guest entering the Hawleys' house in January might have seen them with their children, all twelve or under, working and playing near the warm hearth. Baby Sophia would be sleeping in a cradle or someone's arms. Rufus's parents, Timothy, seventy-eight, and Rachel, sixty-seven, might be there. Married almost fifty years, they lived nearby on the west side of the Farmington River, close enough that Rufus could cross over the river and bring them wood.

Deborah Hawley's nieces Ruth Pomeroy and Katherine Granger and Rufus's sister Abigail Hawley might have been there, too, for without grown daughters, Deborah relied on these unmarried relatives for help. In return, she may have taught them decorative needlework and tailoring. The older Hawley boys—Timothy, Rufus, Jesse and Washington—were also useful. They fixed fences and fetched wood, and Timothy, at twelve, was old enough to escort Ruth Pomeroy all the way to Suffield when her visit ended.

Deborah Hawley was often at her husband's side, welcoming and entertaining relatives and guests, attending funerals and weddings, visiting and going to Farmington. Their farmhouse operated as a childcare center, nursery, restaurant, bed-and-breakfast, pastor's office and parish hospitality center. In this one year alone, the Hawleys had approximately 125 visitors, including a parlor full of young ladies who "came to bring in their yarn," a gift to Deborah.

The entertainment of fifty overnight guests this year seemed to be nothing out of the ordinary for Rufus and Deborah. The pastor also made two hundred visits to homes in the parish, house to house, often arriving unannounced. He spent thirty nights away as he "din'd," "sup'd" and "conversed on religion." Enjoying hospitality in other homes, he "drank Tea" and "took tea," a custom special enough to warrant mention in his journal after the lean years of the American Revolution.

Hospitality was always in good supply at his house. In June, twelve ministers and several other men came for an association meeting and lecture. Rufus sounded proud that "my House" was filled with distinguished friends. He mentioned the presence of two Yale graduates new to their parishes: Reverend Nehemiah Prudden (Enfield) gave the prayer and Reverend Nathaniel Gaylord (Hartland Second Society) delivered the sermon.

The weather this year was alarming. During a January snowstorm, Rufus scrambled to keep his animals safe. "Hail'd & Snowd all Night; very windy: indeed the Storm was very distressing. I was busy taking Care of my Creatures &c." Then came February's flood, which may have reached his farm. With the Farmington River's ice breaking up and the rain pelting down, he called it "the greatest flood that has been for 13 years I Sepose." The river rose so high that Rufus could not cross the bridge near his house to get to the west side. Determined to see people who could not reach the meetinghouse, he decided to cross the swollen river.

Rufus's description of this endeavor is spare: he rode his horse to the Cider Brook area, got a boat and sailed over. On the west side, he walked to a friend's house, borrowed a new horse and rode to Captain James Lusk's on Lovely Street to deliver a religious lecture. He spent the night at Asa North's, and the next day, with water receding and the ground almost bare of snow, he called at most of the other houses on Lovely Street. He returned to his home on the east side of the river that evening.

The high water had been dangerous and destructive, but it also left behind nutrients for the fields. At Rufus and Deborah's farm that summer, friends helped with hoeing, and one July day thirty-two helpful men reaped four and a half acres. There was a killing frost on September 3, but Rufus still picked corn into mid-November.

Along with water and frost, disease threatened Northington: smallpox, diphtheria and scarlet fever. To help prevent smallpox, Dr. Joseph Wells set up a smallpox inoculation center at the secluded Farmington farm of Josiah Kilbourn Jr., the site of today's legendary Hospital Rock with its carved initials of patients. After being inoculated at the farm, people stayed on for a few weeks in isolation until they were no longer infectious. Later on, the Hawley family would find a reason to use a smallpox recovery house closer to home.

The year 1783 was also remarkable because of what Rufus called "the outpouring of the Spirit" in Northington. The spirit was apparently pouring out of other congregations as well. In response to the quickening religious fervor, Northington held a public fast on June 18. Underscoring the significance of this Fast Day was the presence of Reverend Timothy Pitkin (Farmington) and Reverend Samuel Stebbins (Simsbury), and Rufus wrote with satisfaction of that religious service being "very generally attended."

Popular in-home religious meetings began in February and continued all year. On approximately thirty different occasions, Rufus visited homes to lecture, pray, read and converse, including those of Stephen Darrin, Ambrose Hart, the widow Phebe Hart, Captain James Lusk, Elisha Miller, Sergeant Job Miller, Captain Jonathan Miller, Asa North, Barnabus Thompson, Lot Thomson, the widow Thomson, Ezra Willcox, Josiah Willcox, Sergeant Elijah Woodford and Josiah Woodruff. There were also gatherings in the meetinghouse, at Rufus and Deborah's home, and on the road. Supporting his colleagues as they supported him, Rufus attended fast services in other parishes.

The year concluded with a public Thanksgiving in December. Rufus's sermon on faith and victory, from Psalm 98:1, was a message relevant both to the spiritual outpouring and to America's victory over England. Sophia was taking her first steps, and her father had led Northington's deeply spiritual year. The river's powerful flood was perhaps on his mind this New Year's Eve:

Time no more yn [than] *a Stream is at a Stay,*
the flying year is ever on her way
Its gone, an everlasting adieu,
To this, & all before it too.

7

DID BUT LITTLE

Love and Loss, 1784–1790

1784

MARCH 3 Wednesday very cold, & Snow'd most of the Day. did Chores & read. I am this Day 43 years old. It being leap year bring it on the 3ʳᵈ Day.

OCTOBER 29 Friday cloudy & cool. Attended the Funeral of Father. Mr Pitkin pray'd wt us on the Occasion. Uncle Forward, & Brother Hawley were present; who rode for home after the Funeral, as did uncle Hawley, & other Friends

The spirit continued to pour out in 1784. In January, Rufus and his colleagues Ebenezer Gay, Nathaniel Gaylord, Nehemiah Prudden and David Rowland attended a service at the West Suffield meetinghouse to implore the spirit to keep the revival going. Rufus also helped the new religious fervor along by attending over a dozen religious meetings in Northington homes this year, "unless prevented by Sickness."

At his own home, there were worries. One snowy day in late April, Sophia became ill. Rufus managed to go out in the hail and cold rain to get "some Herbs to make a Syrup for Sophia." Sophia recovered, and her father did not write of her again for eight months.

It was Rufus's father Timothy Hawley, age seventy-nine, who was causing the most concern. Timothy had been so poorly that Rufus had come home early from an association meeting in Southington "on acco't of Fathers being

Sick." For three weeks, he had been going to his parents' house on the west side of the Farmington River to gather their wood, pray and keep watch; he spent all of October 27 there, with his mother also ill. Timothy Hawley died that night, and Reverend Timothy Pitkin prayed at the funeral two days later. Rufus did not mention the presence of Deborah or his mother at the funeral.

In his will of 1781, Timothy Hawley left his widow Rachel half of his estate, one good cow, six sheep, a side saddle and ten pounds of money. He also provided for his daughters Abigail Hawley and Deborah Hawley Gleason, leaving each one-quarter of his moveable estate and personal estate and one-third of his money at the Hartford loan office. To his son Thomas Hawley, he gave his share of the Simsbury sawmill irons that he owned with other partners, drag teeth from the sawmill, sleigh irons and the auger that Thomas already had in his possession. To his "beloved son Rufus Hawley," Timothy left all of his outdoor moveable estate that remained and one-third of his money at the Hartford loan office. He considered only one grandchild in his will. To namesake Timothy Hawley, age thirteen, he gave his firelock gun, which was light, reliable and relatively accurate. Young Timothy could hold it with both hands, take a firm aim and fire with confidence.

Sophia Hawley turned two years old in November, a little girl in a sea of six brothers. On a cold Thursday, December 9, 1784, in handwriting as clear as that of the day before, Rufus wrote, "This Morg my Daughter Sophia fell into a Kettle of boilg Milk, & was Scalded from about the middle of her Body almost all over to her feet. I attended up on her a.m."

After caring for Sophia that morning and keeping watch at her bedside, he managed to preach an afternoon lecture at Asa North's. He returned home, and as the season's first snow fell the next day, he "Help'd take Care of my Child." Rufus never mentioned the presence of a doctor. Two days after her accident, on a fair and pleasant Saturday, he managed to write that "this Morning Sophia Died about the Same time of Day that she was Scalded. Did but little of any thing."

The very next morning, a cold and cloudy Sunday, he preached; this must have been what the parish expected. Without using notes, Rufus preached extemporaneously from the book of Hebrews 11:7 of Noah's faith leading him to build an ark to save his family. Sophia Hawley's funeral was that same Sunday afternoon. Reverend Timothy Pitkin came out again from Farmington: "Mr Pitkin came & prayed with us on the Occasion." Rufus's brother Thomas missed the funeral but arrived the next day from Turkey Hills "to mourn with us." Rufus never mentioned Sophia again in his surviving journals.

Middle and foreground: headstone and footstone of Sophia Hawley (1782–1784), daughter of Reverend Rufus and Deborah Hawley, inscribed, "Valued thee not to whom related or by whom begot." *Background*: headstone of Deborah Hawley (1739–1798), stone carving by Calvin Barber, the region's most popular carver. Cider Brook Cemetery, Avon, Connecticut. *Photograph by Peter Wright, 2010.*

Sophia was laid to rest in Cider Brook cemetery near her grandfather. Her headstone, now barely legible, read: "Sacred to the Memory of Miss Sophia Hawley Daughter of Rev'd Rufus & Mrs Deborah Hawley who died of a scald Dec 11 1784 Aged 2 years & 23 days…valued thee not to whom related or by whom begot." This utterly surprising quotation chiseled on the stone speaks of how her parents and brothers loved her. It begs the question, however, of exactly to whom Sophia was related and who really was her father? This curious headstone inscription is not a Bible verse, nor does Rufus explain it in his journal.

Was Sophia adopted? The church vital records, probably written by Rufus, record that he and Deborah were her parents. Adoption was rare in the Northington baptism records for 1751 to 1861, which list only 1 child out of 631 as adopted, except for that one perplexing entry about a "Lone Girl." However, if after six boys, the chance came for Rufus and Deborah to raise a baby girl, they might well have seized the opportunity. Could Sophia have been the illegitimate daughter of Deborah's niece Sophia Pomeroy of Northampton, Massachusetts, almost seventeen at the time of little Sophia's birth? Whatever Sophia's origins, the Hawleys showered her with love, and Rufus referred to her as "my child" and "my daughter."

Rufus kept busy. That same dreadful week of Sophia's death, he left Deborah and the boys for two nights to attend a church council meeting in Turkey Hills. The ministry of his friend Aaron Booge was in trouble. Back home on Sunday, he preached morning and afternoon from the book of Samuel 3, a chapter that had nothing at all or everything to do with his daughter: "Let God do what seems good." A week later, Rufus left a clue about Deborah Hawley's own grief when the women of Northington stayed with her and helped with sewing. Her husband wrote how "a Number of Ladies came this Day to give Mrs Hawley a Spell of Sowing; Some all day, & Some p.m."

Where was Rufus's soul searching, his grief, his fury over the accident? Characteristically, he did not use his journal to state his emotions or describe anyone's feelings. Even in his heartbreak, he recorded just the facts. If his emotions are to be found anywhere, it is in his sermon texts and in the journal's annual closing words. On December 31, he preached a Friday Sacramental sermon asking God to give light to those in darkness and in the shadow of death and to guide them to peace. The verse summarized the past year perfectly: a religious awakening stirred Northington, and the Hawley family was desperately seeking solace.

Rufus concluded this journal with words from Isaac Watts's 1719 hymn, "Our God Our Help in Ages Past." The full verse is: "Time, like an ever rolling stream, Bears all its sons away; They fly, forgotten, as a dream, Dies at the opening day." Shortening it for New Year's Eve, he must have been thinking of his daughter:

Time Like an ever rooling Stream,
flies Swift away Just like a Dream.

1785

MARCH 4, Friday cheifly cloudy, but thaw'd. read & Studied I am this Day 44 years old.

APRIL 7 Thursday cloudy & fair alternately. went with Rufus to Mill with a Sled. freezes hard Nights, So yet in ye Morning it is Good walking on the Snow, & yt Snow is a foot deep or more, I Sepose, in open Land, & near 2 feet deep in ye woods. People of all ages Say, they don't remember ever to have known Such a Body of Snow on the Ground at this Season of the year before.

Somehow, life went on. There was a new singing master at the meetinghouse, and at one Thursday afternoon session, David Gleason learned five new tunes. Captain William Woodford had been working at the meetinghouse, putting in more seats and stylish balcony wainscoting.

"Rufus Hawley Ejus Ephemeris, or Journal, Jany 1st Anno Domini 1785." Translation: "Rufus Hawley His Diary, or Journal." *Hawley-August Collection of the Avon Free Public Library.* Photograph by John Pecora.

The Hawley family's grief this year can be found in quiet clues on the pages of his journal. In one of the rare entries referring to God, Rufus was grateful when several women came after a snowy night to help Deborah with sewing. Needing a change of scene, perhaps, in mid-February Rufus took Deborah, Washington, 8, and Orestes, 7, on a ten-day trip through northern Connecticut and Massachusetts, visiting those who could provide sympathy and tender care: brothers, sisters, uncles, cousins, and friends. They stopped at the home of Deborah's sister Sybil Kent Pomeroy, the mother of the teenage Sophia Pomeroy, and at Belchertown to see Justus and Violet Forward.

After this trip, Rufus went to Turkey Hills to sit on a council considering the future of the discontented Reverend Aaron Booge, who had been pastor there since 1776. Reverend Booge had asked the Turkey Hills Society for dismissal, but the people of Turkey Hills "manifest[ed] a great & genl unwillingness" to dismiss Reverend Booge, wrote Rufus. The council persuaded him to stay another year and to try to live "peaceably & happy" and "advised ye People to Strive to make him contented." Aaron Booge did not last the year, for in December the Council dismissed him, said Rufus, as there was "little prospect of his further usefulness."

Another pastor asked for dismissal this year. Reverend Timothy Pitkin, Farmington's pastor for over thirty years, had lost his congregation's support when he stopped using the Halfway Covenant to baptize children whose parents were not church members. On a hot June 15, the issue came to a head when Rufus attended the council meeting in Farmington with Northington delegate Dr. Solomon Everest.

After the ministers met at Reverend Pitkin's home for the midday meal, they gathered at the meetinghouse. Rufus gave the opening prayer. After hearing Reverend Pitkin's reasons for dismissal, which Rufus said was for "want of Health principally," the council went to Reverend Pitkin's house and formed its response. Rufus wrote that the councilmen returned to the meetinghouse, where they dismissed Pitkin: "[We] went to the meeting-house, read the result, in which Mr Pitkin was desmis'd, then Mr Upson made a Prayer and Mr Smally preach'd a Sermon &c After which the Council dispers'd." The dismissal of Rufus's colleagues shows the frailty of any minister's hold on his own pastorate. After sixteen years in Northington, Rufus's theology, reputation and strength were still holding up.

According to custom, the Connecticut General Assembly met in Hartford, in May, to count the votes from the spring elections and to elect representatives.

During the weeklong celebration, citizens practiced their military skills and enjoyed social visits and special foods. Rufus went to Hartford for election day on May 12, when dignitaries met at the Connecticut Statehouse grounds and walked to the Hartford meetinghouse. The Governor's Foot Guards led the parade, followed by Governor Matthew Griswold and dignitaries and then by about one hundred ministers and the Governor's Horse Guards. The meetinghouse service opened with a prayer and hymn singing and a sermon by Rufus's Yale classmate, the epileptic and eloquent Reverend Dr. Samuel Wales.

That summer, for perhaps the only time in the journals, Rufus mentioned playing with his sons. On June 22, he "spent the day" at Cherry's Pond (today Secret Lake) fishing with Timothy, Rufus, Jesse and Washington and with Lieutenant Foot and his sons. They "spent the day." Back at work during the fall harvest, Rufus spent four days carting grain and a week cutting hay in his meadow. He finished picking corn in November. December marked a year since Sophia's death:

May the fleeting of time,—put me in
Mind,—to improve wt is behind.

1786: NO JOURNAL

Reverend Justus Forward's diary once again sheds light on Rufus's concerns this year. In Turkey Hills, Justus's widowed mother (Rufus's aunt) Mercy Forward suffered an "apoplectic fit" and was near death. Upon receiving the news, Justus rode approximately six hours from Belchertown to Turkey Hills, where "Mother [was] so low that I did not speak to her." The next morning, he "spoke to my Mother, she knew me...but could not speak so as I could understand her."

Justus stayed in Turkey Hills for ten days, preaching in the pulpit vacated by Reverend Aaron Booge. A spring storm "grew tedious," and Mercy Forward "gradually declined." Soon after Justus went home to Belchertown, Mercy Forward died. Instead of returning to Turkey Hills for her funeral, Justus attended a four-day church Council meeting of ministers in Granby, Massachusetts. The council members, he wrote, needed him in Granby, and they "judged that I was called in Providence to stay here."

Of Northington's ten deaths this year, 50 percent had been children. There had been twenty-seven births, about average, and the pastor performed twenty baptisms, including the daughter of Ensign William and

Esther Woodford. Fanny Woodford was another child whom Rufus would probably never forget.

1787

DECEMBER 15 Saturday fair, very windy & quite cold. Studied. Timothy R. went to Turkey-hills to teach a School.

DECEMBER 27 Thursday fair & very pleasant for Winter. Having been invited, by Letter from the Secretary of the Lodge of Freemasons, to attend on their Exhibitions at Farmington this Day; I went: Mr Smally preach'd a Sermon; Capt Mix (one of the Freemasons) deliver'd an Oration, &c, &c. After Exercises, walk'd with the Masons to Mr Solm Cowles Jr, & dind with them. there were 9 Ministers present.

News came in late January from Springfield, Massachusetts, that farmers, led by Captain Daniel Shays, had violently disrupted the courts and attacked the Springfield armory. Several had been killed, wrote Rufus on January 26, after they "rose in a Mob to prevent the siting of the Court." For several months, Shay's Rebellion and the crisis of farmers in debt had gripped the region.

But smaller worries also passed through the Hawley home. He recorded a flutter of irritation on a summer Sunday when Deborah's nieces Maria Kent and Ruth Kent stopped on their way from Suffield to "the Sea Side." Ruth Kent was "very poorly" and hoped a few days by Long Island Sound might improve her health. Uncle Rufus seemed alarmed not at her health but rather with the young women traveling on a Sunday. He was "not pleas'd at all with their Journeying on the Sabbath Day."

A minister's meeting this year merited only a brief mention in the journal, but it brought Rufus into the company of Reverend Lemuel Haynes, age thirty-six, pastor of Torrington and a man who would become famous in the history of the United Church of Christ. On that rainy morning, Rufus and Reverend Jeremiah Hallock (Canton Center) rode to Reverend Samuel Mills's meetinghouse in Torringford for "public services" and the meeting of the Hartford North Association with Joshua Knapp, Alexander Gillett and Abraham Fowler. The other minister present, noted Rufus routinely, was his colleague Reverend "Hayns" of Torrington.

Lemuel Haynes was born in West Hartford, the son of a Caucasian mother and an African American father. Abandoned by his mother as an

Reverend Lemuel Haynes (1753–1833), colleague of Reverend Hawley and the first African American ordained in any denomination. Born in West Hartford, he was raised as an indentured servant from infancy to age twenty-one by Deacon David Rose of Granville, Massachusetts. Pastor of Torrington, Connecticut (1787–1789), and Rutland, Vermont, for thirty years, Reverend Haynes also worked for the Missionary Society of Connecticut in Vermont and New York. *Collection of the Connecticut Historical Society, Hartford, Connecticut.*

infant, Lemuel was raised and educated by a church deacon and his family in Granville, Massachusetts. Young Lemuel worked on the farm as an indentured servant until he was twenty-one years old. Ordained in 1785 by the Litchfield County Association of Ministers, Reverend Haynes was

Connecticut's first African American Congregational pastor. After serving as Torrington's pastor for several years, he was pastor in Rutland, Vermont, for thirty years.

During the bountiful summer of 1787, some of the Hawley boys were old enough to have their own responsibilities but still needed help from their father. In July, he "help't the Boys burn the further Field." The family reaped a plentiful rye crop in July and spent two weeks harvesting hay and collecting bundles of rye and wheat. "We have this year (thro' a kind Providence) 115 or 116 Shocks of Rye & 13 Shocks of Wheat. In the whole 128, or 129 Shocks. May we be duly thankfull."

The harvest was satisfactory, as was the church attendance of two men long absent. On the first Sunday of September, Rufus wrote proudly how "this Day Capt Jonathan Miller, & [his son] Mr Elisha Miller, who have call'd themselves Churchman ever Since I was ordain'd in this Place, return'd to this Chh." As Rufus had recorded in his journal fifteen years before, the Millers had lost three family members within two days in 1772. Their return to church was perhaps prompted by the declining health of Captain Miller, age eighty, for he died two months later on a rainy Thanksgiving morning.

Yale's commencement in September was of unusually keen interest to Northington's pastor, for one of the graduates, Publius Virgilius Booge, age twenty-three, had started his studies with Rufus at age eight. Rufus arrived on Tuesday, September 11, in time for prayers in the college chapel and "attended on Commensment" the next day. He spent that evening with other ministers at Reverend Dr. Samuel Wales's house; on Thursday, he attended the traditional Conscio ad Clerum (advice to the clergy), a gathering the day after commencement where a minister, selected three months earlier at the General Association's annual meeting, gave a sermon. Rufus then rode home to Northington with "several Gentlemen's Company part of the way."

In December, Rufus and Deborah's eldest son, Timothy, age sixteen, left to teach school in Turkey Hills. His cousin, Edward Eugene Hawley, later described him as tall, handsome, active and cheerful. Timothy taught school for the next fifteen years, volunteered to help with Northington's library and was treasurer of the Third School District.

Timothy's departure in 1787 left five brothers still at home: Rufus, fourteen; Jesse, thirteen; Washington, ten; Orestes, nine; and Zerah, six. The boys' help around the farm was recorded by their father: moving dirt around the house's foundation, gathering wood, helping build hovels and leading sheep home. After a Christmas Eve snowstorm, Rufus and young Rufus broke a path to the mill through knee-deep snow.

The year ended on an intriguing note, when Northington's pastor attended a Freemasons' meeting in Farmington. The Freemasons had established their lodge only three months earlier but labored, like all masons, under the suspicion of being a secret society conspiring against Christianity. Inviting local ministers to attend meetings was a way to obtain a valuable stamp of community approval. Never one to miss a meeting, Rufus found the Freemasons thoroughly agreeable.

The final page of this year's journal contains a list of thirty-eight library books that Rufus had read. On the list were religious books and collections of sermons; books of poetry and a book on Captain James Cook's voyages to exotic lands. There were histories of the American Revolution, Ancient Greece, Iceland, Florida and Massachusetts, along with Jonathan Edward's *History of the Work of Redemption*.

It seems unlikely that Rufus ever started a sermon with a joke, for *The American Jest Book*, he sniffed, was "not worth reading." It is hardly surprising that the man who rejected perhaps the only joke book in Farmington ended his year lamenting how

> *the Year role's away;*
> *And Man returns to Clay.*

1788: NO JOURNAL

Connecticut's missionary movement began in Rufus Hawley's own Hartford North Association this year, when the ministers approved a plan to send missionaries for ten weeks into "new countries," far-off mission fields such as New Hampshire and Ohio. Rufus's colleague, Reverend Dr. Nathan Perkins (West Hartford), accepted a post in Vermont.

Four years after this, in 1792, the General Association of Connecticut's Congregational churches would adopt a statewide missionary program. After the formal establishment of the Missionary Society of Connecticut, in 1798 missionaries would serve in New Hampshire, Pennsylvania, Ohio, Vermont, Indiana, Mississippi Valley, Kentucky, Indiana, Virginia, Tennessee, Iowa, Michigan and Louisiana. From 1834 to 1848, it turned out, Missionary Society ministers and money had to hold together a struggling new church in a nearby mission field: West Avon, Connecticut.

1789

OCTOBER 22 Tuesday fair & hot. read, & work'd Some. Katharine Granger went home, who has liv'd with us every since the 10 of Jany last.

NOVEMBER 15, DD Fair & moderate. preach'd fm Gen. 18 [verse missing] *a.m. & administered the sact. & p.m. partly an old Sermon, & partly extempore; & baptized Alma, a Child adopted by Sister Spring. She is Daughter to Abel Hawley.*

Timothy Hawley was young and ambitious, and as the son of a minister with five brothers, unlikely to receive a large inheritance. Seeking a better life than what he could find in Connecticut, he left Northington just prior to his eighteenth birthday on a three-month trip to what his father called "Genesee Country." Western New York would hold a strong attraction for Connecticut migrants when thirty-five million acres of surveyed land in Genesee County, New York, went up for sale in 1801. For now, however, Timothy returned home for the fall harvest and to teach school at Pleasant Street (today Country Club Road). His trip west, however, had opened up a world of possibilities.

The Hawley house still never lacked for visitors. A warm April afternoon found Rufus studying until the "Ladies" arrived to drink tea, bringing in "yarn wh they had given us the Spining of." Ministry candidates from Yale paid their respects: Gad Newell (Yale, 1786) of Southington would be pastor in Nelson, New Hampshire. Ebenezer Kingsbury (Yale, 1783) of North Coventry would be a missionary in New York and Pennsylvania and pastor of Jericho, Vermont. Also visiting for extended periods and making themselves useful were Deborah's nieces Katharine Kent Granger, about twenty-one, of Suffield, and Isabel Phelps, about twenty, of West Springfield, Massachusetts, who stayed for five months.

Orestes Hawley, age ten, was old enough in May to help his father take their sheep to pasture in Hartland; Rufus and young Rufus, age sixteen, retrieved them five months later on a snowy day in late October. The journals record the comings and goings of the Hawley sheep with regularity, and these sheep are representative of a thriving Connecticut wool industry. In Hartford, Rufus could have found a ready market for his wool at Jeremiah Wadsworth's Hartford Woolen Manufactory, established the previous year and the first woolen mill in the United States. Wadsworth bought wool from Connecticut farmers, and he paid cash.

Every day brought surprises: sons in and out, spinning ladies, candidates popping by, sheep on the move. The public's interest in religion also was surprising this year, reminiscent of the parish's spiritual stirrings in 1783 and 1784. During what he called a "great awakening in these parts" on June 17, Rufus went to Salmon Brook to preach a service with Reverend Jonathan Miller and Reverend Israel Holly. Meanwhile, Gideon Curtis, age thirty-seven, died in West Simsbury (today Canton). He left behind his widow, Elizabeth, four young sons and a baby girl. What would happen to Mrs. Curtis might become Rufus's biggest surprise of all.

On a raw and windy Tuesday night in October, Rufus performed the marriage of his sister, Abigail Hawley, age forty-five, of Northington to Thomas Spring of Granby. Mr. Spring, a widower in his early fifties with a houseful of children, now had a new and helpful wife. A month later, Rufus baptized a child that Abigail had adopted, Alma (or Almira) Hawley, about six and the sixth child of Rufus's cousin Deacon Abel Hawley. What led to this adoption is unknown, with the pastor writing only that he baptized the girl, who was "a Child adopted by Sister Spring."

8

Life's a Dream

Books and Antislavery Sentiments, 1790–1797

1790

OCTOBER 3 *DD Cloudy & raind a little preach'd at Barkhemsted. Mr Eels at Hartland, Mr Gaylord at Simsbury, & Mr Stebbins for me. This Evening Timothy Ruggles was married.*

DECEMBER 2 *Thursday cloudy & exceeding cold. rode to Mr Stebbins; made a Short Stop; then to Brother Hawley's & dind, then to Newgate, & took a view of the prison; then to Mr Gad Taylor's of Suffield, & lodg'd. Jesse went with me, & Ruth Granger; they went to Brother Grangers.*

Rachel Hawley, a widow for five years, moved into her son's home on a "pleasant" day in January, and Rufus wrote that he "help'd bring Some of her Household Furniture to my House." This day was doubly important because "Mother came to our House to live" and Thomas Spring of Turkey Hills "took home" his wife, Abigail Hawley. Rufus had performed his sister's wedding four months earlier, and the newlyweds were now following the custom of going to housekeeping weeks or even months after the ceremony. The bride's brother, Thomas Hawley, held a "friendly Social Evening" for the couple and their guests. It was quite unlike the party one might expect today. "A Hymn was Sung," wrote Rufus, "& upon Desire I made a Prayer."

The next day, perhaps to care for Rachel Hawley, a revolving lineup of relatives began living with Rufus and Deborah. Along with his mother, other women also took Rufus's attention this year. He visited and prayed with his friend Mrs. Damaris Booge Northway, "exercis'd with fits." Syble Hart, age eighteen, and Sabre Hart, twenty-four, were "under Concern," Widow Ruth Thomson had a shock of the "num Palsy," and Mrs. Zelpha Thomas suffered "great distress of mind." Among the men in the parish, Samuel Gleason was terribly ill. Rufus visited this elderly neighbor regularly and preached a lecture in February at Samuel's house two months before his death. The pastor also preached or attended lectures at the homes of Mrs. Lucy Darrin, Sergeant Elnathan Hart, Sergeant William Porter, Lot Thomson and Josiah Wilcox. Riding through his parish, Rufus could easily spend an entire day in "religious Conversation with Some people" or a forenoon "conversing upon various religious Subjects."

Rufus was not the only person going house to house. To compile the United States' first national census this year, a census taker had to visit every household. On the Farmington enumeration list, the names of Northington residents are in a cluster, indicating 115 households and 575 people: 1 slave, 176 free white males ages sixteen and older, 170 free white males under age sixteen, 226 free white females and 2 "free persons." Three women were household heads: Mary Andrus, Zelpha Thomas and Ruth Thompson.

Rufus Hawley never described his views on slavery, but there are clues in the journals to his experiences and antislavery outlook. Farmington's 1790 census recorded six slaves living in five households. Rufus had dined with Suffield's Reverend Ebenezer Gay Sr., who owned five slaves, and according to a 2009 study by Robert Romer, it was not uncommon for Massachusetts ministers in the Connecticut Valley to own slaves. Rufus was also close to men who worked against slavery. His teacher at both Hatfield Academy and Yale had been antislavery writer Reverend Ebenezer Baldwin. Reverend Baldwin and Reverend Jonathan Edwards Jr., pastor of New Haven's First Church and one of America's most important antislavery orators, had written articles for the *Connecticut Journal* condemning slavery. Rufus probably heard Dr. Edwards's 1791 speech on the slave trade. Most importantly, Dr. Edward's book, *The Salvation of All Men Strictly Examined* (1790), listed Reverend Rufus Hawley's name as a subscriber.

Connecticut's first antislavery association formed this year in New Haven: the Society for the Promotion of Freedom and Relief of Persons Unlawfully Holden in Bondage. Its president, Ezra Stiles, was also president of Yale. The society's members were Congregational ministers and laymen dissatisfied with Connecticut's slow and limited efforts at emancipation. Connecticut had passed a law allowing black and mulatto children born after March 1, 1784, to be free at age twenty-five, and the society supported more antislavery efforts.

Rufus Hawley joined up immediately and was in good company. The society's 153 members at this time included Noah Webster and many of Rufus's colleagues: Reverend Benoni Upson (Berlin), Reverend Samuel Mills (Torrington), Reverend Nathan Strong (Hartford Center Church), Reverend Nathan Perkins (West Hartford), Reverend Allen Olcott (Farmington), Reverend Theodore Hinsdale (North Windsor) and Reverend Dr. John Smalley (New Britain).

Two years later, at the 1792 General Election in Hartford, Rufus heard what he called an "Oration against Slavery." Accompanying him that day and presumably helping to spread more antislavery news through the Farmington Valley parishes were Reverends Samuel Mills, Jeremiah Hallock (West Simsbury, today Canton) and Abraham Fowler (Reverend Hallock's predecessor in West Simsbury). Rufus's opposition to slavery must have influenced his son Orestes's own actions. Years later, Orestes and his wife, Polly, would use their home in Ohio as a station on the Underground Railroad.

After eighteen years in their first house on the east side of the Farmington River, near the meetinghouse, Rufus "mov'd with my Family over the River" in May. This is the first mention of a new house, but he owned more than one hundred acres on the west side of the Farmington River and had spent time running boundary lines with a surveyor. The previous year he had built a new cow house and lean-to there. The move was interrupted in September when he returned from a four-day meeting in Wintonbury (Bloomfield) to find that "my Family had mov'd back to the East Side of the River" because the house still needed work. Rufus helped the joiners and did lathing, and when the plasterers finished the two front rooms in early October, he swept out the lath, shavings and sand and brought his family back. This would be their home for the next nine years.

An accident on the Farmington River led to an unusually long journal passage on May 20: "In the morning the dead Body of a Man was found in the River (by Mr. Gleason's boys) near against the Meeting house. It was suppos'd to be the Body of Benjamin Beckwith, who was drowned on the 21st of April last, near Mr. Aaron Woodruff's. the father of sd Beckwith, & 2 of his Brothers, (upon word being Sent them) came in. they Suppos'd it to be him; desir'd me to make a Prayer, wh I did; & the body was buried."

Mabel Beckwith, however, said that the clothes on the body were not her husband's, and because she did not own "the cloaths that the body had on that was found yesterday…a Number of People who live near where he did, came & dug up the Body, & became satisfied that it was not his and who it is, no mortal can tell at present." Benjamin Beckwith's body was soon found above the mill in Farmington.

Another mystery appears in the journal on October 3, when Rufus wrote that "this Evening Timothy Ruggles was married." There was not even a pointing finger in the journal to mark the day when Rufus and Deborah's eldest son, age nineteen, married Northington resident Deborah Ingham, age twenty. The line was squeezed into the text as an afterthought. Rufus did not write the place of the marriage or the bride's name, nor did the Hawleys attend the ceremony. That day seemed more memorable to Rufus for preaching at a four-way pastor exchange. Seven months later, Timothy would bring "his wife home to live with him" in Northington, following the custom of going to housekeeping. Timothy and Deborah would have nine children and move to the Western Reserve in 1802.

Of pressing concern this year was finding an apprenticeship for Jesse Hawley. The tall boy had physical strength, a genial disposition and sound judgment. He was also illiterate. When Jesse turned sixteen years old in December, Rufus took him in a sleigh to Suffield to see Gad Taylor, a merchant who took in apprentices to learn blacksmithing. Jesse immediately joined the Taylor household of twelve people and was bound as an apprentice the following April "to learn the blacksmith trade." He stayed for about two years. Jesse's illiteracy begs the question of what kind of education he had received in Northington. In contrast to Jesse, the achievements in higher education of his brothers Orestes and Zerah would be quite extraordinary.

On December 5, the Sunday sermon in Northington was on having faith that God will care for one's children. Deborah and Rufus had let go of Jesse just a few weeks earlier.

1791

Sept 15 Thursday a very rainy Day attended the consio ad Clerum in the Chappel, preach'd by Mr Day; a Lector preach'd by Dr Edwards in the Brick Meetinghouse to the Society for ye Promotn of Freedom &c. and a Meeting of Sd Society. Then rode to Mr Wm Love's & lodg'd.

November 9 Wednesday Cloudy & moderate, & towards Night & in the Evening raind considerable. Dr Everest & I rode to New-haven in a Chair to buy Books for the public Library

The Journals of Rufus Hawley, Avon, Connecticut

At his half-century birthday on March 4, Rufus wrote, "This Day I am 50 years old." The warm weather left "open Land" half bare, and he delighted in seeing robins and bluebirds. A few weeks later, he and Deborah invited forty-three women who had done their spinning to their home for a social time. There was tea to drink, and Rufus "waited on [the] Ladies." The women's yarn was a gift to Deborah, age fifty-one, for she had not done much of her own spinning lately.

In January, Deborah had become "exceedingly exercis'd with pain." She was able, however, to take a ten-day journey to visit friends and family, riding to Simsbury with Rufus and Washington, fourteen, and Zerah, nine, to see Reverend Samuel Stebbins. Her trip continued with Washington taking "his Mamma" to her brother John Kent's house in Suffield. Riding north to Southampton, Rufus preached in the Southampton meetinghouse, and they celebrated the marriage of Deborah Hawley's sister Ruth to Southampton's pastor, Jonathan Judd. Their final stop on the way home was at Newgate Prison.

After doing his chores on a snowy April 7, Rufus was called to a crisis: William Woodford's daughter, Fanny, age four, was "dangerously sick," and he was needed immediately to pray with the family. Rufus knew them well, for William Woodford had lost his wife, Esther, age forty-two, the year before and his daughter Janey, fourteen, in 1786.

Writing in his journal two days later, Rufus did not flinch describing his visit to the Woodford house to see "the Doctor open his Daughter Phanny who died yesterday. Upon examinatn, it was found that one part of the Intestine was folded, or doubled into the other, So that nothing could pass through. Return'd home, read Some, & p.m. attended the funeral of Phanny Woodford. pray'd." This autopsy was unusual enough to warrant the pastor's presence and his long journal entry.

William Woodford would need his pastor again, for with several young children to look after, he could not stay a widower for long. On August 4, Rufus performed his marriage to Mary North of Northington. Their daughter, Fanny, was born seven months later.

On May 16, an earthquake measuring 4.3 on today's Richter scale shook parts of Connecticut. The epicenter was Moodus, forty miles from Northington, where chimneys toppled, stone walls collapsed and there were fissures in the ground. Rufus wrote only of noticing "two shocks of Earthquakes in the Night."

Today's Avon Free Public Library had its beginnings on September 26, 1791, when Rufus rode through Northington "to get Subscribers for a Library." On October 6, he "attended a church meeting, & a Library

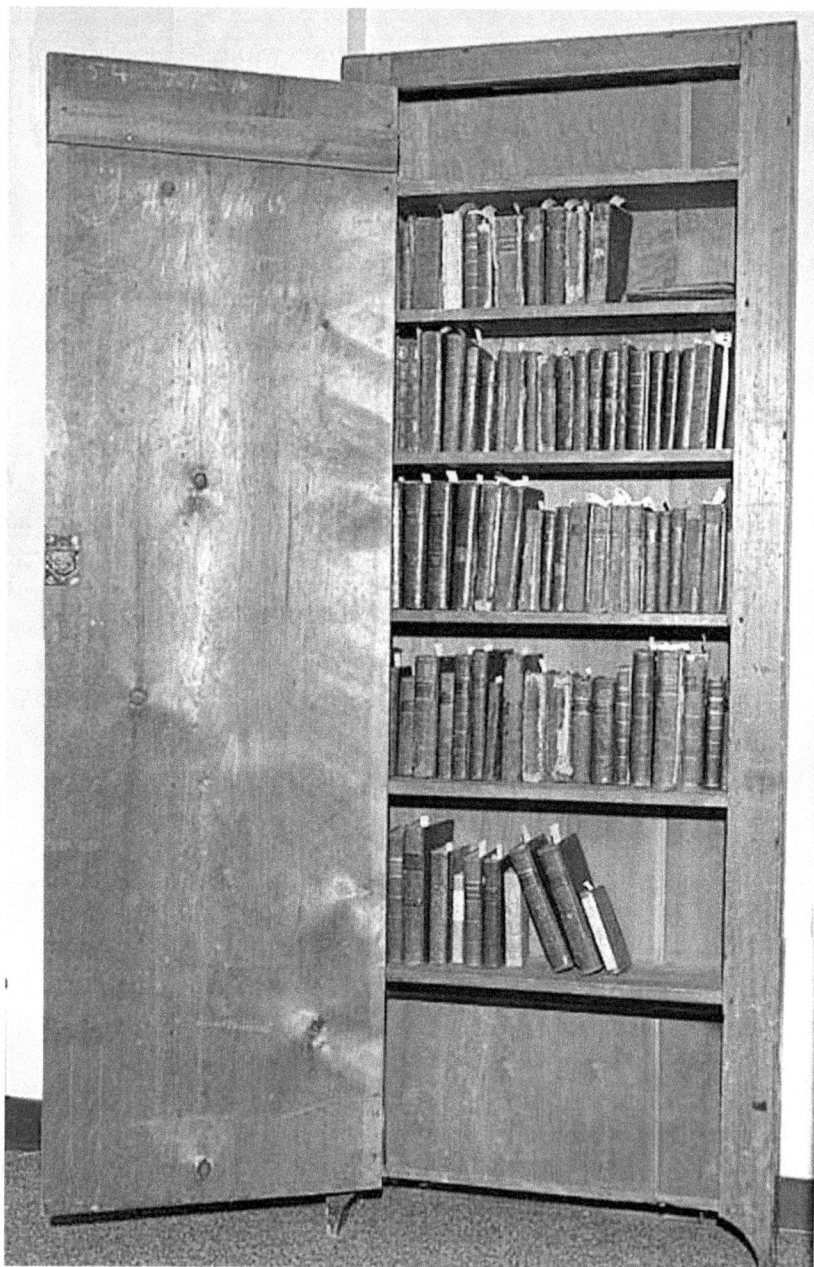

On November 10, 1791, Reverend Rufus Hawley and Dr. Solomon Everest "purchased books" in New Haven to establish Northington's library. In 1971, the Wilcox family donated ninety-six original books listed in the 1798 Northington Library catalogue and the original book cabinet (by tradition designed to fit on a wagon) in memory of Harold Wilcox, grandson of Ansel Wilcox, Avon librarian from 1842 to 1853. *Collection of the Avon Free Public Library. Photograph by John Pecora.*

meeting at ye Meetinghouse." Five weeks later, with money to spend from the parish, Dr. Everest and Rufus went in a carriage to New Haven on November 9. They spent the night and bought "books for the public Library;" the next day, they "purchased Books and rode home." Back in Northington on November 11 and eager to get started, Rufus "did Errands, Set up Library &c." While Rufus did not write where the library was located, it was probably at his home.

As the library's treasurer, Rufus collected dues and membership fees to pay for purchasing more books. By 1798, when Northington's library catalogue of 121 books was printed as a broadside, the collection had novels, poetry and books on travel, history and biography. There were mathematics and philosophy books, a book on catching whales off Greenland, Daniel Defoe's *Robinson Crusoe*, Adam Smith's *Wealth of Nations* and Benjamin Trumbull's *History of Connecticut*. The forty-seven books on religion constituted the majority of the collection.

For the next ten years, Rufus regularly attended bimonthly library committee meetings in February, April, June, August, October and December, at which times library subscribers had access to the books. He did not hesitate to write short book reviews in his journals: "This book is very poor" and "this book is not worth reading."

The antislavery momentum of the previous year continued, and in September, Rufus attended a meeting of the Society for the Promotion of Freedom and for the Relief of Persons Unlawfully Holden in Bondage. With ministers and dignitaries already in New Haven for Yale's commencement, it was convenient for the society to meet and to hear Reverend Dr. Jonathan Edwards Jr.'s sermon on *The Injustices and Impolity of the Slave Trade*. This printed sermon is one of the earliest antislavery publications in the Library of Congress.

As the year concluded, Rufus and Deborah must have been thankful for their first grandchild. Ruggles Hawley was born in August to Timothy and his wife, Deborah, three months after Timothy "brot his wife home to live with him." In December, however, a reminder about the loss of Rufus and Deborah's daughter Sophia came on a bitterly cold Thursday. Lucy Tillotson, about four, the daughter of Ashbel and Phebe Tillotson of Lovely Street, had been walking to school when she fell and drowned in the brook west of her house. Had she fallen through ice? Did another child run for help? Rufus attended Lucy Tillotson's funeral the next day, December 7, only four days before the seventh anniversary of Sophia's accidental death: "Time flies man dies."

1792

*OCTOBER 21 DD Cloudy a.m. clear'd off p.m. cool & windy. preach'd, &
attended the Funeral of Mr. Appleton Woodruff's Wife; who died yesterday
morning. the Corps was brot to the Meetinghouse, & prayers made there.*

*DECEMBER 19 Wednesday Went with Washington to Major Church's of
Springfield. Left him, with a view to have him learn the hatter's trade.*

Something was terribly wrong with Deborah Hawley. In April, she stopped
going to the meetinghouse and was too ill to return for seven months. Her
husband does not describe her condition or whether it was a disease in her
body or mind. She was so "very poorly" that the women of the neighborhood
did her sewing, and her husband took what must have seemed a desperate
measure. In late May, he had Deborah "electeris'd" by Dr. Solomon Everest.

Electric shock treatment had been gaining acceptance since the 1760
publication of John Wesley's *Electricity Made Plain and Useful by a Lover of
Mankind and Common Sense.* The day after Deborah's electric shock treatment,
Rufus and their son Washington left her and rode to West Suffield to Reverend
Daniel Waldo's ordination. It seems odd that Rufus spent that night away
from Deborah, but he returned in time to take her back to Dr. Everest's
three days after her first electric shock treatment. She continued to see the
doctor, one week, two weeks and six weeks after that. Her husband tried to
take good care of her, getting medicine and finding roots to make a "strong
beer." He took Deborah out for rides and visits almost daily and brought her
to the schoolhouses to hear children recite their religious lessons.

Perhaps the strongest indication of Deborah's fragility was an event
that happened only once in the journals: Rufus took her to the Yale
commencement. This meant four days away from home, and he needed
help to manage the visit. Rufus Forward Hawley, age nineteen, met them
in New Haven and must have been of assistance, for at no other Yale
commencement did Rufus mention the presence of a son. Deborah walked
with her husband "to the waterside"; they saw friends, marveled at the
evening "Illumination" and attended "the Meeting for the abolition of
Slavery." They heard lectures by Reverend Theodore Hinsdale of North
Windsor, Reverend Dr. Levi Hart of Preston and antislavery leader
Reverend Dr. Jonathan Edwards Jr. of New Haven.

Two of the other Hawley sons would not have been able to get away
from their jobs to help with their mother. Both were working as apprentices

in Suffield, Jesse learning blacksmithing at Gad Taylor's and Washington learning hat making at Timothy Swan's. Washington lasted at his apprenticeship only about five months and came home on November 3, "not to return to Mr Swan's again." Six weeks later, on a cold and snowy day in December, a possibly frustrated Rufus Hawley took Washington to Springfield, Massachusetts, to Major Moses Church's and "left him there with a view to have him learn the Hatter's Trade."

Moses Church had been taking in hat making apprentices at least since 1766, when Justin Hickcox, age fourteen, of Granville, Massachusetts, had signed on for an indenture of seven years. If Washington Hawley's terms of training were similar to what is printed in Justin's indenture, Washington kept his master's secrets and agreed to his master's rules of behavior. He did not play cards, swear or frequent taverns. In return, Major Church taught him "the trade Art of mystery of Hat making & to Read write cipher" and provide "good Sufficient meat Drink Lodgings wearing Aparrel & washing and Provide for Him two suits of Apparril."

At year's end, with Deborah's poor health and their sons growing up, Rufus could not shake that uneasy sense of time passing. He once again turned to Isaac Watts for inspiration in writing his New Year's Eve words:

> *Time like an ever roleing Stream,*
> *Sweaps man away, his life's a Dream.*

1793: NO JOURNAL

If Rufus's journal from 1793 had survived, it might have had a finger pointing to two events: the birth of his second grandchild, Imri Judd Hawley (son of Timothy and Deborah Hawley), and the move from Farmington to Northumberland (today Moreau), New York, of cousin Amos Hawley, age thirty-eight. This move west must have been galvanizing to the five of six Hawley sons who would one day seek opportunities away from Connecticut: Timothy, Orestes, Washington, Jesse and Zerah.

In the Northington account book of Preserved Marshall, a picture emerges of Rufus and Deborah buying necessities and niceties: linen, calico, muslin, thread, a fan, a silk handkerchief and four quarts of rum.

1794

FEBRUARY 5 Wednesday Fair, very windy & extream cold. The Associatn Spent the forenoon in religious conversatn, broke up p.m. I rode home. Married Jesse Willcox of Northington (Widoer) & the Widw Comfort Peck of Bristol.

APRIL 10 Thursday fair & quite cold. Rode round over the River to invite the Ladies to give Mrs Hawley a Spining spell.

On January 5, Rufus admitted his son Timothy and Timothy's wife, Deborah, to full communion in Northington. Left unsaid was what took so long for them to join the church and why they waited until Sunday, May 11, four months after this, to have Rufus baptize Ruggles, almost four, and Imri Judd, ten months.

On a cold and rainy day in February, Rufus performed the marriage of widower Jesse Willcox of Northington to the widow Comfort Peck of Bristol. It was an ordinary event for Northington, but part of that wedding is today extraordinary: the bride's dress of brown silk survives in the collection of the Avon Historical Society.

Another especially meaningful baptism took place this spring at the home of Samuel Hart. After Reverend Edward Griffin (Yale, 1790) preached a lecture there, Rufus baptized the five children of David and Lois Hart Bristoll: David, Adna, Sarah, Ery and Lois. It seemed an unusual event, baptizing five children at once at a home with two ministers present. But Rufus was accustomed to doing unusual things for the couple. In 1771, they had awakened the pastor at midnight to perform their marriage.

An unusual entry in David Gleason's *Day Book* recorded that a Baptist minister preached in the Northington meetinghouse, an event that seemed entirely acceptable. Reverend Rufus Babcock, who also was ordained this year, founded Colebrook's Baptist Church and had a long ministry.

In April, four years after moving to the west side of the Farmington River, Rufus purchased more property there. He swapped five acres of his land in the Meadow for five acres from Jesse Willcox. He also paid 600 pounds for nineteen acres and for David Gleason's house, barn and cow house. The Farmington River was his eastern border, and perhaps he could look across to see the meetinghouse.

The Hawleys moved into Gleason's former house on April 29, 1794. Nine months later, on a pleasant day in December, Rufus brought his clock from the old house to this new one and set it up. A bit of a mystery is that David Gleason reserved ownership of the south part of the house that belonged to Abigail Gleason, his wife—half of the south room, half of the chamber and half of the cellar. A year later, in August 1795, Rufus paid ten pounds for this part of his house.

Rufus's widowed sister, Deborah Hawley Gleason, lived on his southern border, and he bought her seven acres or so in 1797. The Hawley land records in the Farmington town clerk's office show continual activity during this time and more activity when his sons began to purchase and sell land. These records also illustrate how the parish was known by different names: "Northington Parish," the "Society of Northington" and "Northington Society."

On Sunday, August 10, Rufus Hawley wrote of performing an ordinary wedding, with the difference being that the groom did not have a last name: "Rode to Town & preach'd. Mr. Edmund Porter preach'd for me. Rode home, & in the Evening I married Richard, a Negro, of Newington, & Abigail Brawton, a Molatto" of Farmington.

In December, his twenty-fifth anniversary as Northington's pastor, Rufus preached his "quarter of a century Sermon." On that cloudy and rainy Sunday, he reminded the congregation of the foundations of their faith.

This New Year's Eve, his thoughts may have turned to milestones and the coming of justice:

> *The wheels of time role on apace,*
> *and man fleets Swifly on his race.*

1795

APRIL 6 Monday Fair & very warm a.m. clouded up p.m. and raind Some in the night. Rode to Town [Farmington] *a.m. attended Library meeting p.m. The Ladies who have given us a Spining Spell, came to bring in the yarn, & drink Tea wt us this afternoon. there were 63 present.*

SEPTEMBER 24 Thursday fair most of the day & cool. work'd at hay. In the evening married Rufus F. Hawley (my 2d Son) & Betsey Richards.

The day after the Northington library's February meeting, David Gleason wrote in his *Day Book* that he and Timothy Hawley rode in the rain to Hartford to buy more books. "Early in the morning I put in our old horse and Tim. Hawley and we go to Hartford. Git 15 Books for the Library, with the Librarian money cash of L 4:19-4…We go back 1 hour by Sun, attend Library meeting." One of the new books for what Rufus called the "Library Company in Northington" was a collection of sermons by Rufus's colleague Nathan Perkins.

The Hawleys' farm also was growing, as Rufus purchased more land and got a cow. In April, he framed a cow house and corn house and raised the two structures two days later. He rode to Newgate Prison to obtain nails and fretted over a July drought. After two weeks of "extream" and "exceeding" hot days, a "plentiful" shower brought relief, and in a rare show of emotion, Rufus gave praises for "this rich mercy." Hard rain continued to fall, and August brought two floods.

The Hawley sons still needed their parents' attention. The September wedding of Rufus Forward Hawley, twenty-two, tall and thin with a large aquiline nose, received that pointing finger in the journal. Zerah, fourteen, lived at home and helped his father drive sheep to pasture in Barkhamsted. In May, Rufus took Orestes, sixteen, to teach at the academy in Salmon Brook, and Orestes, seventeen, taught in Hartland later that year.

In June, Rufus went to Hudson, New York, on a four-day trip. He delivered clothes to Jesse, twenty, who as it turned out had already sailed to New York City a few days before his father's arrival. Jesse had caused concern a few months earlier after a pay dispute with his former employer, blacksmith Theodore Bidwell of Farmington, and his father had to settle the matter. At year's end, Jesse left for Albany, New York.

Timothy, twenty-four, a schoolteacher in Farmington, presented Rufus and Deborah with their first granddaughter that summer. "Had a Grand Daughter born," he wrote. The baby's name honored a sister that Timothy had known for only two years. On a fair and pleasant Sunday, Rufus "baptized Sophia Daughter to Timothy R. Hawley."

George Washington Hawley, eighteen, seemed to vex Rufus the most. Three years into an unhappy hat making apprenticeship at Major Moses Church's in Springfield, Washington was legally bound to stay until he turned twenty-one. Rufus took clothes to him in May, but Washington returned home in early November. His father took him right back a week later. With no resolution, the matter was put to arbitrators, who recommended that Rufus pay Major Church twenty-five pounds for the lost time that Washington would not serve. "I setled wt Majr Church" was Rufus's crisp entry. On Christmas Day, Rufus arranged for Boan King, a hatter of Westfield, Massachusetts, to take Washington as an apprentice.

Years later, Edward Eugene Hawley described his uncle Washington as five feet and eleven inches tall, strong, active and morose.

The state of religion in Northington may have vexed Rufus as well. At a midweek service on a "cold, windy, Squally Day" prior to Sunday's communion, "there were So few present, that I did not preach: only made a Prayer." But several ceremonies boosted his spirits. When peach and apple blossoms bloomed in May, Rufus gave "the consecrating Prayer" at the Farmington ordination of Reverend Joseph Washburn. At Reverend Edward Dorr Griffin's ordination in New Hartford, Reverend Dr. Jonathan Edwards Jr. gave the sermon, and Rufus gave a lecture and the customary "right hand of fellowship." Reverend Griffin would go on to be president of Williams College.

Rufus's attendance at Yale's commencement had special significance that fall, as it included the inauguration of the college's new president, Timothy Dwight. True to form, the journal provided few details. "Put up at my old Landlord James Bradley's. Walk'd to College, attended Lector in the Brick [meetinghouse], the Inauguration of President Dwight in the Chapel, Illumination, &c."

On a bleak New Year's Eve, foggy weather and melting snow exposed the brown landscape. Rufus ended the year with perhaps the gloomiest New Year's Eve lines he ever penned:

> *Year after year is roleing away*
> *And man is mouldering down to clay.*

1796: No Journal

Shopkeeper and parish postmaster Preserved Marshall obtained his license this year to keep a tavern for strangers, travelers and others and to sell alcohol. Conveniently located at Nod Corners at the base of Talcott Mountain, the Marshall Tavern was the parish post office and a popular stagecoach stop with overnight accommodations, refreshments, liquor, a ballroom, sheds for carriages and barns with stalls for resting and switching horses. The location was perfect for business, for three years later, the Talcott Mountain (or Albany) Turnpike opened, directly linking Northington to Hartford and to the gateway west: Albany, New York.

1797

JANUARY 27 Friday fair & thawd fast. Raind considerable in the night. Visited Timothy's & Orestes's Schools.

JUNE 5 Monday fair & warm. Did Chores, wrote & attended Library Meeting. Too day I sold my House & land on the East Side of the River.

Timothy Hawley's third son, Chalker, was born in August and baptized by his grandfather three weeks later. On a cloudy Friday soon after, Rufus "Pray'd wt my Grandson, Chalker Hawley, who died p.m. Studied & wrote." That Sunday, as usual, Rufus was in the pulpit preaching.

Rufus's mother, Rachel Forward Hawley, eighty-one, was of constant concern. Although Rufus had recorded that she moved in with him in 1790, he also said the same this year that this time Rachel seemed to stay the rest of her life. Reverend Justus Forward visited and noted in his journal that one of the Mrs. Hawleys was "quite poorly." He could have meant either Rachel or Deborah.

This year Rufus sold his former house and farmland on the Farmington River's east side. After Jesse returned from Ohio, Rufus helped his son obtain items to set up his own blacksmith shop by getting tools in West Simsbury and stools in New Hartford. Orestes taught school in Southampton, Massachusetts, and then began studying medicine with Dr. Solomon Everest. Zerah Hawley, sixteen, started two years of religious studies with Reverend Joseph Washburn in Farmington.

Settlers were beginning to move from Connecticut to northern New England and the Western Reserve (also known as New Connecticut) and needed pastors. Rufus, clearly supporting an effort to send Connecticut missionaries to serve these new communities, read aloud to his congregation one Sunday from "a Pamphlet respecting missions." A few years later, in 1807, at the Hartford North monthly meeting in Torrington, Rufus heard Reverend Jeremiah Hallock (West Simsbury, today Canton Center) speak of his own missionary work in Vermont and the Western Reserve.

Rufus did what he could in the face of injury and disease. "Visited & pray'd with Capt. Samll Bishop p.m. who has been kick'd by a horse, & his life endangered." He spent a day collecting alms for Ithuel Hamlin, who was "sick at his house with the Consumption;" he visited Captain Ichabod Norton, who fell from the new Nod bridge, which broke down soon after it was completed. Deacon Levi Thomson needed a visit, "in Some measure

Reverend Rufus Hawley's journal, December 31, 1797. Words adapted from a hymn by Isaac Watts (1674–1748): "Our moments fly apace/nor will our minutes stay;/Just like a flood our hasty days/Are sweeping us away." *Hawley-August Collection, Avon Free Public Library.* Photograph by John Pecora.

derang'd in mind." After Sarah Miller suffered a stroke, Rufus stayed with her all night until she died at sunrise. He undoubtedly heard of a tragedy narrowly missed by Justus Forward, who wrote in his Belchertown journal how "my House took fire on the Roof, and by divine goodness, was soon extinguished." A few bright spots emerged this year, however, more noticeable for how rarely these kind of entries appear in the journals. In August, he went with Deborah to eat watermelons at Mr. Northway's, and in October, he got a bag of peaches at William Porter's.

New Year's Eve, once again, was a time to remember that time passed too quickly and to borrow more lines from Isaac Watts:

Our moments fly apace,
Our feeble Powers decay,
Swift as a flood our hasty days
and Sweeping us away.

9

I Awoke This Morning

Heartbreak and Happiness, 1798–1799

1798

SEPTEMBER 26 Wednesday fair & pleasant. Busy a.m. attended the Funeral of Ruggles & Imri p.m. Mr Washburn preach'd.

OCTOBER 19 Friday fair a.m. cloudy & raw p.m. Did chores rode to Majr Willcox's & dind, to old Mr Spencers, & drank Tea wt Mrs Curtiss & others. rode home in the Evening.

Rufus Hawley now owned 157 acres in Northington, along with his dwelling house on the west side of the Farmington River and eighty rods immediately surrounding his home. The federal government exempted his property from taxes, calling him a "Minister of the Gospel" in the 1798 U.S. Treasury Direct Tax list. During the twenty-eight years he and Deborah had lived in Northington, they seemed to have built a comfortable life together.

Deborah Hawley had been infirm for years, and the journal indicates that when they went to bed one Saturday night, nothing seemed amiss. Indeed, the *Connecticut Courant* reported that she had "retired to rest as comfortable as usual." Rufus described what happened next. On Sunday, April 8, "when I awoke this morning, I found my dear wife dead by my side. Mr Robert Porter preached for me. I attended." Barely missing a beat, he also went to a Freeman's meeting the following day in Farmington. After dining with his friend Reverend Joseph Washburn, he "Rode home & mourned."

Headstone of Deborah Kent Hawley (1739–1798), Reverend Rufus Hawley's wife, expert needleworker and mother of seven children. The *Connecticut Courant* called her funeral a "melancholy occation." Rufus Hawley purchased the headstone in Simsbury in 1802 and installed it at that time. It reads, "Consort of The Rev. Rufus Hawley who Died April 8 AD. 1798 Aged 58 years…The memory of the Just is Blessed." Cider Brook Cemetery, Avon, Connecticut. *Photograph by Peter Wright, 2010.*

Deborah's funeral was Tuesday, and the *Connecticut Courant* recorded that "there were six Ministers present" and "a large and respectable concourse of real mourners." Reverend Jonathan Miller (Burlington) prayed, and Reverend Samuel Stebbins (Simsbury) preached a sermon from the book of 1 Corinthians, verses 56 and 57, "adapted to the occasion," noted the *Courant*. Rufus wrote that "a number of other relatives & a large concourse of other people came to console wt us on the melancholy occation."

Rufus installed his wife's expensive headstone four years later, in Cider Brook Cemetery, near their daughter Sophia's headstone. It reads, "Consort of The Rev. Rufus Hawley who Died April 8 AD. 1798 Aged 58 years. She made a profession of Christianity in her youth & has left ground of hope, that She is happy with God. The memory of the Just is Blessed." The *Connecticut Courant* also noted that Deborah had "fulfilled the duties of all the relations she sustained," she had been Rufus's "beloved partner" and her husband, her "afflicted friend," was left with "the consolation of a full persuasion that she is now blessed in the enjoyment of heaven."

Two weeks after her funeral, Rufus wrote that he "helped Timothy move to my house." What Rufus did not mention was that, along with his son Timothy, age twenty-six, the family must have come, too: his pregnant wife Deborah, twenty-seven; Ruggles, six; Imri, four; and Sophia, two. Among the friends visiting at this time of upheaval to offer condolences was Reverend Dr. Jonathan Edwards Jr.

When Rufus returned after a three-day trip to Massachusetts in September, he was alarmed to find Zerah, age seventeen, "sick." Three days later, with Zerah "sick wt the Dysentary," he could not leave home, "prevented from going to Commensment [at Yale] by Zerah's Sickness." For the next six weeks, Rufus wrote about the scourge. "Rode to Elijah North's & pray'd with his oldest son, who died Shortly after. Their other Son died last week. Pray'd wt 2 of Lt. North's Daughters, who are Sick"; "attended on the sick & dying in the a.m. John Ingham lost a child Thursday and Samuel Norton lost one Wednesday"; "visited the sick child of John Ingham's"; "attended the funeral of James Smith's child"; "prayed with Mr. John May's sick child"; "Linus Hart's…daughter Emelia died about noon today, aged 16 months."

Then, on September 24, the journal reveals what Rufus must have feared all along: "Monday fair & comfortable. My Grandson Imri Hawley died about 9 o'Clock a.m. of the dissentary. Taken up a.m. attended upon the sick & dying." The next day, Rufus wrote, "Tuesday fair, very windy. My grand son Ruggles Hawley died about noon of the dissentary. He was 7 years old, & Imri 5. Attended to him a.m. rode to Town p.m. attended a Lector preach'd by Mr. Fenn. mother & Zerah have had the dissentary but are recovered."

Ruggles and Imri's infant brother, Chalker, had died the year before; the headstone for the three children reads, "Heaven has confirm'd the great decree That Adams race must die: One general Ruin sweeps them down, and low in dust they lie." That Sunday, Rufus's sermon from Psalm 90:5, 6 was on life's brevity.

Then, against all odds, the tone of the 1798 journal became hopeful. Three months after Deborah Hawley's death, the entries whisper about the widower's social life bursting with possibilities. Visits to Roswell Spencer's house to drink tea sound uneventful, but Mr. Spencer may have been present only as a courtesy while Rufus courted widow Elizabeth (Betsey) Mills Curtis of West Simsbury (today Canton Center). During the first visit to Mr. Spencer's on July 12, Rufus does not mention Elizabeth, but the date was one he clearly wanted to remember: "Rode to Mr Rosel Spencer's, & Slept."

According to the journal entries, Rufus and Elizabeth married on what was their seventh visit. On November 13, the groom "rode to Rossel Spencers & was married to Mrs. Elizabeth Curtis (widw) and return'd wt her, her daughter Betsey, & her goods." The following day, he "assisted in setting up Mrs Hawley's furniture."

Elizabeth Mills Curtis Hawley, a widow for ten years, had four grown sons; her daughter Betsey was ten years old. Burt's *Early Settlers of West*

Simsbury called Elizabeth "uncommonly kind and agreeable," and "it appeared to be a settled principle with her, that whatsoever god did was right." Rufus had known her father, the late Reverend Gideon Mills of West Simsbury, and young Elizabeth knew her father's colleague. When Elizabeth was young and her father had to stop work because of cancer on his face, neighbors and the General Association had donated money to his family. Rufus had stepped into his pulpit, "he being in a declining state & unable to preach." At Reverend Mills's death in 1772, Rufus and Deborah had quickly gone to console the family; Deborah had stayed to make mourning clothes.

After Rufus's devastating losses this year, life seemed almost routine at year's end. He did his chores, read, visited and prayed with people, performed marriages and entertained visitors. In November, his grandson Thales Hawley was born, son of Timothy and Deborah, who had so recently lost Ruggles, Imri and Chalker. On the day of "Publick thanksgiving," Rufus preached from Psalm 30, which seemed to describe his family this year: weep but rejoice in the morning.

The day after Christmas, Rufus and Elizabeth hosted a party with about twenty neighbors. "Deacns Joseph & Elijah Woodford, Capt. Dudley Woodford, Ensign Obadh Gillet, Messrs Isaiah North, Samuel Phelps, Perez Marshall, Elijah Miller, Samuel & Selah Woodford, their wives, & the wife of Isl [Israel] Woodford, come to See us. They bro't plenty to eat & drink." He sounded happy that night, but on New Year's Eve he turned melancholy:

This year my Wife rent from my Side,
And Grandsons two have also di'd,
Which teaches me I Soon must go,
to realms of bliss, or realms of woe.

1799

November 2 Saturday fair, windy & raw. Very busy. My chimneys were finish'd. Orestes went to ye westward.

December 13 Friday cloudy & cold. Rode to Mr Joseph & Gad Hawley's & din'd, then home & attended an adjourn'd Library meeting. We dissolv'd our Liby, & divided the Liby & company into 4 Devisions.

The Journals of Rufus Hawley, Avon, Connecticut

The Hawley sons were now grown. Jesse, twenty-four, married Lydia Hart in May. Washington, almost twenty-two, with his failed apprenticeship behind him, had joined the army and was encamped in New Haven when his father paid a visit. In September, Rufus and Orestes went to New Haven to see Zerah, eighteen, who had entered Yale after studying with Reverend Joseph Washburn for two years. "Rode to New-haven p.m. Orestes went wt me. Zerah went yesterday, & this day entered a Colledge." Zerah had perhaps attained his height of five feet and eleven inches by now and had dark brown hair, blue eyes and thick eyebrows. Orestes, twenty-one, trained in medicine, left Northington in November for a five-month trip to "ye westward." Tall, stout and robust, Orestes had enormous muscles, broad shoulders, dark brown hair and gray eyes and was described years later by his nephew as a "wonderful" man. Elizabeth's son Gideon Curtis visited Northington, and Rufus called him "our son."

This year, education and commerce in Northington took two strides forward. The Northington Library committee arranged the library so that borrowing a book was much more convenient by dividing the books among four different homes. Samuel Bishop (at 7 Bishop Lane) and three other unidentified caretakers made the books available to subscribers and collected fees with which to buy more books. Travel also became more convenient with the opening of the Talcott Mountain Turnpike (Route 44). Northington was on the main highway between Hartford and Albany, New York.

Northington was also in the midst of another spiritual revival, the Farmington Valley's version of the Great Awakening fifty years earlier. Thomas Robbins wrote in his diary on April 17 that "the awakening at Hartford still continues... It also spreads in Wethersfield, Farmington, Simsbury."

The event was so astonishing that Rufus wrote about it in the *Connecticut Evangelical Magazine*, a firsthand account intended to be read at religious meetings and passed among friends. Describing Northington's "remarkable" scene and "the whole awakening," he marveled that "there was now a great shaking among the dry bones." His journals reflected his excitement: he frequently attended religious meetings in homes and schools, and gave lectures at the meetinghouse. He was preaching more than ever before and sometimes extemporaneously.

This year, Rufus may have tried to visit almost every one of the approximately 137 households in the parish. In May, he rode to Lovely Street and "call'd at every house & convers'd wt the people upon relg [religion]." Forty to fifty people joined the church, and he baptized thirty children in two weeks. "The service of God is now sweet and pleasant to them," he wrote in the *Connecticut Evangelical Magazine*.

The Reverend Rufus Hawley House (1799), 281 Old Farms Road, Avon. *Wick Mallory Photograph, 2011.*

Rufus and Elizabeth were also "very busy" with building their new house (today 281 Old Farms Road), facing east on a hill overlooking the Farmington River. On July 11, a fair and pleasant day, Rufus wrote that he "had a house rais'd. Spend the day attending to the business." This was the fourth house that Rufus had owned in Northington. Friends helped dig and cart stone, and he rode to Suffrage (today Canton Center) for boards and to West Hartford for nails. The chimneys were completed in November.

The first floor of the house had two rooms facing the road and two side-by-side kitchens to the rear. This unusual arrangement was perhaps forward-thinking, planning for the day when Rufus and Elizabeth would need others living there to help take care of them. Rufus was beginning again, in his fourth house in Northington. The Hawley land eventually would encompass today's Stony Corners, Stony Corners Circle, Avonside, Avonside Knoll, Hawley Hill and both sides of Country Club Road from Rails to Trails to Tamara Circle.

10

MY SONS AT NEWCONNECTICUT

The Western Reserve, 1800–1811

1800

*JANUARY 16 Thursday cheifly cloudy & thawd. waited on visiters, &
mov'd into our new house.*

*FEBRUARY 22 Saturday cheifly cloudy, but moderate. Studied, & preach'd
fm 2 Chron. Last clause of the 24, & first of ye 25 Vs on account of ye
Death of Genl Washington. the Society having requested it. Deacn Abel
Hawley came to our house, & tarried over the Sabbath.*

The Hawleys settled into their house at a time when the nation was in
deep mourning. Rufus must have wanted to read with his own eyes the
December 30, 1799 issue of the *Connecticut Courant*, with the notice of George
Washington's death two weeks earlier. The newspaper quoted John Adams,
saying if "prayers could have been answered, he would have been immortal."
Congress set February 22, 1800, for the United States to honor George
Washington's memory. Rufus preached that Saturday from "2 Chronicles,
last clause of the 24, and first of ye 25 Vs on account of ye Death of Genl
Washington, the Society having requested it." This verse concerned King
Amazia, who ruled Jerusalem for twenty-nine years, roughly equal to George
Washington's time in public service from the Continental Congress until
his death. Perhaps Northington's meetinghouse had special music for the
melancholy occasion and two hours of pealing church bells (as in Reverend

Abel Flint's Hartford meetinghouse) or the pulpit draped in black with men and women wearing black crepe or ribbons as badges of mourning (as in New Haven).

In April, there was a brief entry in the journals about smallpox but no detailed description of Orestes, twenty-one, having contracted the dreaded disease. On April 25, Rufus wrote casually and suddenly that he "carried cloathes to Orestes, who has had the Small pox & this day left ye pest house at Mr Thos Fords." A building on the property of Thomas and Hannah Ford's Northington farm had been set aside as an isolated center of recovery for people suffering smallpox, and Orestes was among those who had either come down with the disease or, having been inoculated with smallpox pustules, showed symptoms of smallpox. When Orestes was no longer contagious and free to leave the so-called pesthouse, he must have dressed in the clothes his father brought him and left his old clothes to be burned.

The timing of Orestes's smallpox quarantine is curious, as less than three weeks before carrying clothes to him, Rufus had performed his marriage to Ursula Hawley (daughter of Rufus's cousin Gad Hawley). If Orestes was inoculated, it was perhaps timed to follow his marriage, precede his four-month trip in May to the Western Reserve and make him, in his work as a doctor, immune to smallpox.

Zerah continued his studies at Yale, and in October, when Rufus went to New Haven to settle the bill, he "waited on the President." Reverend Timothy Dwight, Yale's president, still believed that smallpox inoculation interfered with God's design.

1801: No Journal

The tremendous flood that came to Northington this March was the highest one that David Gleason had ever seen in his life. Called the Jefferson Flood for coinciding with Thomas Jefferson's election as president, it destroyed the meetinghouse bridge over the Farmington River. Isolated from his meetinghouse for several weeks, Rufus preached at his house.

Timothy Hawley departed in the spring for the wilderness of northeastern Ohio. Working for the Torringford Land Company of Connecticut, he surveyed and laid out the town of Morgan in the Western Reserve and in payment received land near Rock Creek. Back in Northington, presumably at Reverend Rufus's house, Timothy's wife and children awaited his return.

1802

FEBRUARY 16 Tuesday fair & warm. Read, wrote & attended Singing meeting. Pray'd at the Close. Orestes rode for Newconnecticut.

APRIL 12 Monday fair & comfortable. Timothy, & his family, Chauncey Hawley, wt Orestes's Wife & child, Set out for Newconnecticut. I attended freemans meetg.

The Hawley sons were on the move, and Orestes left Northington again in February for Ohio. Timothy had returned to Northington the previous fall, but only to prepare his wife, Deborah, and their children to move west. On April 12, Timothy, his wife and their children—Sophia, Thales and Almon— left Northington to meet up with Orestes in Ohio. Also with Timothy were Orestes's wife, Ursula, their daughter Cybelia and cousin Chauncey Hawley. They arrived safely in their new home on June 1, 1802. Rufus must have been terribly worried, for when he heard of their safe arrival two months later, he wrote with relief how he had "receiv'd letters from my Sons at Newconnecticut, giving an account of their Safe arrival, with their families. Praised be the Lord." Trying to help from afar, Rufus sent Orestes a "box of medicines" with Reverend Nathan Gillett, pastor of the Gilead Society of Hebron, who was traveling that way in September.

When he journeyed to Yale for commencement in September, Rufus took time on the way to "barter horses" before arriving at landlord James Bradley's and attending two events. One event was at the brick meetinghouse, and the oration by Reverend Samuel Wales was at the "blue meetinghouse." Rufus had never mentioned the Separate Society's blue meetinghouse before, which stood at the corner of Elm and Church Streets and which he knew from his student days in New Haven.

Rufus installed his late wife's headstone and footstone in May. He had ridden to Simsbury "after Grave Stones" and went the following week "to the burying ground to help Set up Mrs. Hawley's grave Stones." On New Year's Eve day, a snow fell "Shoe deep" in Cider Brook Cemetery.

1803: NO JOURNAL

Zerah Hawley had spent four years at Yale College, and this year, at age twenty-two, he graduated with his bachelor of arts degree. Rufus must have attended the ceremony in September in the brick meetinghouse in New

Haven, certainly noticing that the class of fifty-seven men was more than double the size of his own class in 1767.

The move of Hawley relations to the Western Reserve continued when Rufus's cousin Samuel Forward of Turkey Hills moved to Aurora, Ohio. Rufus must have heard about the forty-eight-day journey, with six adults and eight children in two large wagons, one drawn by horses and the other by two yokes of oxen.

1804: No Journal

In 1804, Rufus sent a report about Northington to his Yale classmate John Treadwell, who was compiling information about Farmington and its parishes for a statewide survey of towns for the Connecticut Academy of Arts and Sciences. The academy was a learned society chartered in 1799, and its president, Timothy Dwight, was also president of Yale College. He planned to publish the town reports, and to show the nation that Connecticut was a model of morality. Rufus's job was merely to report about schools, leaving one to wonder why Treadwell had not asked his friend to write about religion.

In what may be Rufus Hawley's only surviving letter, he wrote to John Treadwell that the parish had precisely 170 students, ages four to fourteen, in the Center School, Ciderbrook School and Nod School. These three schools were in various states of repair: poor, "midling" and good. The fourth school, with thirty students from Northington and Farmington, was located on Lovely Street.

He recorded that the school visitors, the two or three men who kept an eye on the teaching and the students, visited the schools twice in the summer and twice in the winter. "They require the Bible to be read at least once a day," he wrote, "by those that are capable of reading it, to be read in a decent sober manner. The catechism to be taught once a week or more; & that the male Instructors pray in the schools, at least once a day." The students learned spelling, grammar, writing, arithmetic, the Bible and the shorter catechism.

Northington schools, he also reported, operated about ten months a year. Male teachers earned $8 to $12 a month for the winter season and paid $1 a week to board; female teachers earned four shillings to five or six pence a week in the summer and paid fifty cents a week to board. He said that Connecticut helped pay the school's annual cost of $304.25 with income from the sale of lands in the "western territory."

Treadwell never submitted this report to the academy. Finally published in 2003, the report on Farmington and its parishes was long, with nine columns about manure and a mere three columns about religion. While Rufus certainly appreciated the value of good fertilizer, he was spared, it appears, from reading about the minor role that religion played in Treadwell's final report.

1805: No Journal

The roadway that passed by the Hawleys' house (today's Old Farms Road) became an official Farmington town road this year, and Rufus, now sixty-four, took to it for what was probably his longest journey so far: over five hundred miles away to the Connecticut mission field of Harpersfield, Ohio, on the shores of Lake Erie. In October, he met there with his friend Reverend Thomas Robbins, who had been sent two years earlier by the Connecticut Missionary Society to organize churches. According to Reverend Robbins's diary, Rufus was present in 1805 at a meeting with Robbins, Reverend Joseph Badger, Reverend David Bacon and delegates from four local churches. The group had formed itself into an ecclesiastical association, and "Mr. Hawley, a minister from Connecticut, attended with us. We were happily united in sentiment."

With his interest in missions, Rufus's journey to Ohio must have seemed the trip of a lifetime. There were also personal reasons to take the journey, for Orestes, Jesse and Timothy lived in the vicinity and Rufus had two new granddaughters: Evelina and Elvira.

1806

FEBRUARY 7 Friday cloudy & cold. visited & pray'd wt Apheck Woodruff, Lt Horsford's Wife, a daughter of Ira Eaton's, Mrs. Frisbie, Ozem Woodruff, Mrs Allyn & Rebeccah. Mr Elmisha Hawley, his wife, & oldest daughter came to our House.

OCTOBER 9 Thursday cheifly fair & pleasant. Rode to Mr Wadsworth's Seat on the mountain, to the raising of a barn, &c.

In 2009, the West Avon Congregational Church sexton uncovered a forgotten headstone lying flat underground in the adjacent cemetery. After the thick grass was pulled back, Elizabeth Frisbee's headstone emerged with only a few words still legible: "—children whose—streaming tears—say not in transport of dispare that all your hopes are fled."

Several times in early 1806, Rufus had prayed with Mrs. Elizabeth Woodruff Frisbie, age thirty. On February 10, he "attended" her funeral, a word he always used by itself to describe his role at funerals, but at Mrs. Frisbie's service, he was moved to describe his role more fully as "praying and exhorting." The family's situation was certainly critical, for Elizabeth Frisbie had died after the birth of her son, and her husband, Amasa, a shoemaker at Nod Corners, could not care for the infant. Elizabeth's older brother, Eldad Woodruff Jr., and his wife, Elna—who had been married thirteen years and seemed to have only one child, Electa—took the baby home. Rufus Hawley baptized David two months later, writing in his journal that David was Eldad Woodruff's "adopted Son" and the "Son of Amasy Frisbie."

There were some delights this year. Rufus noticed "spring birds" and how trees from a distance did "not appear to have buded any." During the peak of fall foliage, he rode to a barn raising at "Mr. [Daniel] Wadsworth's Seat on the mountain," with its grand view of the Farmington Valley from atop

The Reverend Rufus Hawley House, 281 Old Farms Road, Avon, Connecticut. The south side front room was likely the pastor's study, where he may have written in his journal. *Wick Mallory Photograph, 2011.*

Talcott Mountain. He saw a "total eclips" of the sun and enjoyed weather so mild after church in late November that "loose coats & cloaks were not needed." He delighted in working with books as he "assisted in arangeing the Library."

Perhaps feeling his age, one day Rufus "rid round inviting young men to give me a Spell cutting wood." He also rode through the parish a second time asking for help. Orestes, now twenty-seven, had returned to Northington in May, and a journal entry hints at the crisis when his father "rode to lovely-Street beging for Orestes; his house having been burnt." Over the next two weeks, Rufus went out four more times "asking charity for Orestes" and collecting donations.

The three-day General Association meeting in Wethersfield gave Rufus the scholarly company he craved. The ministers dined at the home of Wethersfield pastor Reverend John Marsh and heard sermons by Dr. Benjamin Trumbull (Yale, 1759), a historian and pastor of North Haven, and by Reverend James F. Armstrong and Reverend Samuel A. Clark, both from New Jersey. Dr. Ashbel Green, of Philadelphia's Presbyterian Church, was there, too. Years before, he had fled from that city's infamous 1793 yellow fever epidemic, only to return to perform a funeral and weep in his black-draped pulpit.

At year's end, Rufus served on a council in Simsbury concerning the future of Reverend Samuel Stebbins, who had requested his own dismissal. Helping to finish off the almost thirty-year pastorate of a man who appeared to be his dear friend, Rufus said only that they "desmissed him." Samuel Stebbins, however, noticed with harsh honesty the declining health of his Northington colleague. He thought that a long sermon by Reverend Hawley, "stricken with palsy" and trembling, would never end and that he was "hence not a captivating preacher."

On December 31, there was no special New Year's Eve closing, just the scene of a stepfather worried about his stepdaughter. "Fair and extream cold. Rode to Town on business. Dind at Mr. Porters. Betsy is Sick. We have call'd a Doctr."

1807

MAY 8 Friday. Chiefly cloudy, windy & raw. Read, Studied, wrote & attended the funeral of Su, an Indian woman; who died at Johnson Booth's. Pray'd.

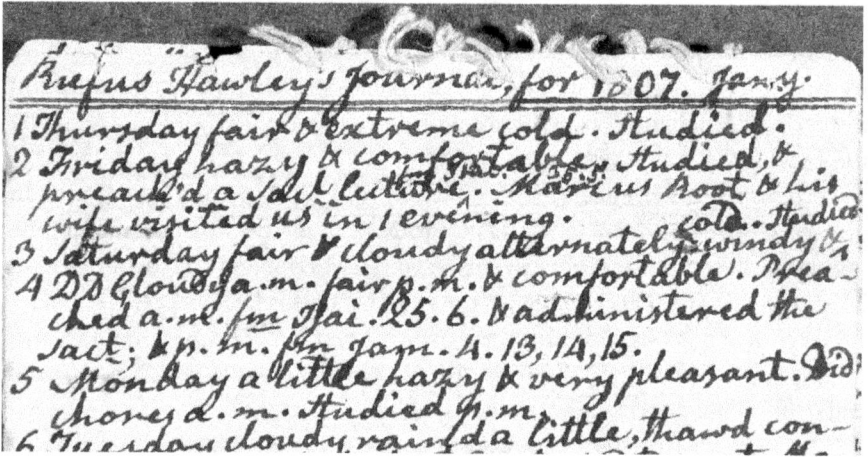

Reverend Rufus Hawley's journal, January 1–5, 1807, showing the way the journals were stitched together at the top. *Hawley-August Collection, Avon Free Public Library. Photograph by John Pecora.*

JUNE 7, DD Fair & quite hot. Preach'd fm Jer. 8.6. all day. Baptized Oliver Norman, & Obadiah Lorman, Sons of Capt Obadiah Gillit: & Willford, Son of Apheck Woodruff.

On a hot Sunday in June, Rufus baptized three baby boys in the aging meetinghouse. Obadiah Gillit brought his two-month-old twins, Obadiah and Oliver, and Apheck and Beulah Woodruff brought their three-month-old son, Wilford. The twins, unusual for Northington, probably got most of the attention that day, but Wilford would one day get international attention. In baptizing the infant Wilford Woodruff and welcoming him to the church, Rufus set in motion an astounding religious trajectory. Wilford spent his youth in Northington and Farmington and then moved west. In 1833, at age twenty-six, he joined the fledgling Church of Jesus Christ of Latter-day Saints (the Mormon Church) and eventually became president of the church's European Mission. He married five and possibly more women, some concurrently, and in 1889 became the Mormon Church's president. The next year, he outlawed polygamy.

Another person whom Rufus mentioned casually in the journal this year stands out: Su, "an Indian woman" who died at the home of Johnson Booth, about twenty-nine, in Northington. By performing her funeral and writing of it in his journal, her pastor left what may be the only record of Su's life. Her name does not appear in the parish death records.

The autumn brought losses to the Hawleys, both in Northington and in Ohio, and both events deserved the hand-drawn finger pointing to the journal

The Journals of Rufus Hawley, Avon, Connecticut

Above: Traditional birthplace of Wilford Woodruff (1807–1898), in Avon, Connecticut, in the Sleepy Hollow section of the Old Farms area. It is no longer standing. Baptized by Reverend Rufus Hawley on June 7, 1807. Woodruff was the fourth president of the Church of Christ of Latter-day Saints (the Mormon Church), from 1889 to 1898 and outlawed polygamy. *Sunrise Farm Collection, Avon, Connecticut.*

Left: Wilford Woodruff memorial stone, Fisher Meadows Park, Avon, inscribed "...He and his parents, Aphek and Beulah Thompson Woodruff, lived in a modest home approximately three-fourths of a mile west of this site on the north side of Old Farms Road on Avon Old Farms School property. Their farm of about 30-acres had a saw and grist mill and a kiln for drying corn." Soccer ball shows scale. *Photograph by Wick Mallory, 2011.*

entry. Maria Hawley, age four, the daughter of Rufus Forward Hawley, died suddenly on September 15. "Rode to Nod & to Town on business. My little grand-daughter, Maria Hawley, was taken with an inflamation in the wind-pipe otherwise the rattles, about 10 O'Clock yesterday & died about half after 10 OClock a.m. today." Soon after, Rufus received a letter from Orestes in Ohio telling him of the death four weeks earlier of Washington's wife, Roxana. Rufus rode the next day to the Farmington home of his cousin Gad Hawley, Roxana's father, to break the news: "Rode to Mr Gad Hawley's a.m. to inform them of the death of their daughter."

1808

JANUARY 24 DD Fair & cloudy alternately, & moderate: there is a great flood, So that we could not get to the meetinghouse: preach'd at my house fm 1 Cor. 3.6. a.m. & Psal. 119 p.m. Read in the eveng.

JUNE 11 Saturday fair & warm. Spent the day visiting, conversing & praying with the Sick.

Rufus Hawley, now sixty-seven, never once complained about wanting a break from his routine, but after preaching on a rainy Sunday in September, he came close: "Favoured wt much freedom all day. Praised be the Lord for his merciful assistance." Another pleasant day was in April, when Zerah returned home from his teaching position on the eastern shore of Maryland. Rufus seemed overjoyed, recording exactly how long Zerah had been gone: three years and four months. In September, Zerah received his master of arts degree from Yale College, but his father did not travel to New Haven for the commencement ceremony. The pastor was needed at home.

It must have seemed as though the world turned upside down that summer, when a scarlet fever epidemic slammed into Farmington. On one single day, June 6, Rufus visited and prayed with twenty sick people. On Sunday, June 12, after praying with the sick almost daily, he "attended the funeral of Apheck Woodruff's wife." Wilford Woodruff, barely a year old and destined for greatness in the Mormon Church, had lost his mother, Buelah, twenty-six.

Two weeks later, Rufus Hawley helped at a Farmington "society fast, on account of the Sore Sickness." On July 4, he prayed with the ailing Reverend Noah Porter of Farmington (who called the disease spotted fever) and with other "feeble people." Reverend Porter's son, Dr. Noah Porter Jr., later wrote

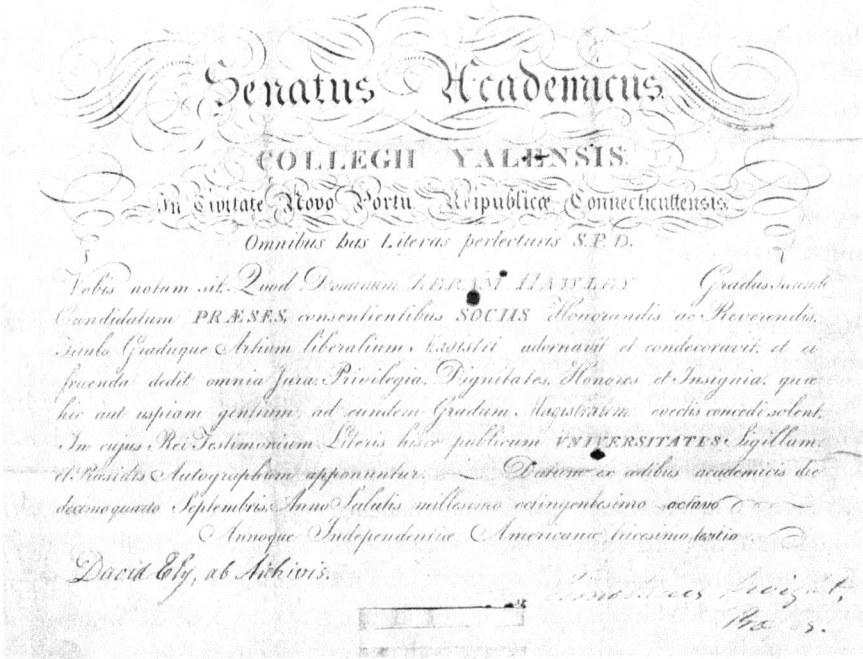

Yale College master's degree of Zerah Hawley, son of Reverend Rufus Hawley, dated 1808 and signed by president Timothy Dwight and David Ely. *Hawley-August Collection, Avon Free Public Library. Photograph by John Pecora.*

how Dr. Solomon Everest and Dr. Eli Todd did all they could in the panic and that the healthy could barely take care of all the sick. The roads were empty, and fearful travelers stayed away. The church bell in Farmington fell silent, for the sound of it ringing once at every funeral had been unbearable. The epidemic lasted one year, striking about seven hundred people in Farmington, many of them women and young children. In Northington, thirteen adults and seven children died this year, a slightly higher number than average.

A letter in November from Timothy Hawley, in Morgan, Ohio, to Reverend Justus Forward in Belchertown gives a view of life on the Western Reserve. "We are here in a new Country," wrote Timothy. "My property is not great but above want. Not in debt…Providence has so ordered events that although my property is small it is the most of any one man in this settlement and consequently have more cash for the use of what I have than it otherwise would be."

In a line that could have been written by his father, Timothy continued, "I have been continually taken up with securing my little crop of corn and other things necessary for the family together with some public concerns that crowd themselves in at this time." Taking the opportunity to drum up business, Timothy asked Justus if he knew of people who might want to settle in Ashtabula County: "Please to direct them to me as I have the selling of several Tracts and that is good and cheap I can acommodate most settlers to their minds." Timothy knew from growing up in Northington what a settled landscape looked like and added about Ohio that "our Country will undoubtedly when cleared and cultivated be very pleasant."

Timothy said in that same letter that Jesse Hawley had lost his wife, Lydia, in August and that George Washington had lost his wife, Roxana, in October 1807. His brothers, Timothy informed Justus, had returned to Connecticut. Jesse took his eldest son, Orestes, about age nine, to live with Reverend Rufus and Elizabeth Hawley and to attend school. Washington took little George Washington, about three, and Julia, about one, to his in-laws in Farmington. Wrote Timothy about this upheaval, "Thus the world is continually changing, and we know not what a Day, or an hour may bring forth." The same can be said of Reverend Rufus Hawley. When he returned home on November 5, after a six-day meeting in Turkey Hills about Reverend Whitfield Cowles, he found that "my sons, Jesse & Washington arrived just before me, wt Jesse's Son & both of Washington's children."

After Zerah came home on November 11, Rufus recorded that "4 of my Sons are now wt. me." He said no more about what had clearly been a tragedy for Jesse and Washington, and for their children. At year's end, Rufus knew he was lucky to be alive: "Blessed be the Lord for all the mercies I have received this year."

1809: NO JOURNAL

Northington had worked itself into a disheartening and complicated mess regarding its worn-down meetinghouse, and since 1805, the church minutes had recorded conflicts about where to build anew. There were strong feelings and long meetings. The pastor, it seemed, was powerless to force a decision.

In December, the society minutes recorded three possible new sites: "a place near the turnpike road, east of Joel Wheeler by the north and south road [today 6 West Main Street], one near the dwelling house of Rev'd Rufus Hawley [near 281 Old Farms Road]" and the "other place near the school house in the middle school district [near today's West Avon Congregational Church]." The society's idea, which proved futile, was to sell "subscription papers" to each proposed site and to locate the meetinghouse in the place receiving the highest sum.

1810

June 29 Friday cloudy & fair alternately, & extreme hot. Went after the Doctr for mother, & preach'd a Sacl lecture fm—Mother died in the night.

August 6 Monday fair & pleasant. Prayd wt Dennis Hart: went to the carding mashine; visited & dind a Mr. Asa North's. tarried long at the mashine waiting for roles.

On a hot day in June, Rufus Hawley, now sixty-nine, went to Deacon Samuel Bishop's house on a desperate errand, for his mother, Rachel, was failing and the church deacon had a supply of wine on hand. The next day was a Friday. Before going to the meetinghouse to preach that day's sacramental lecture prior to Sunday's communion, he brought the doctor to his mother's bedside. There is an indication of what an ordeal this was for Rufus, for when he wrote in his journal about preaching, he could not remember his sermon's Scripture verse.

Rachel Hawley died that night, June 29. Two days later, her son was strong enough to serve communion, but a "Mr. Orsborn" (Rufus could not remember his first name either) gave the sermon. Directly following that service, Rachel Hawley was buried in Cider Brook Cemetery beside her husband Timothy; her headstone reads, "In sure and steadfast hope to rise/And claim her mansion in the skies/A Christian here her flesh laid down/The cross exchanging for a crown." Rufus hoped his mother was in a better place.

"Company" arrived in the days after Rachel's funeral, and Rufus was hospitable. He worked in the garden and fields and wrote to his sister Abigail Spring. And then, less than a week after Rachel's death, Rufus went to Hartford and bought a carriage, writing proudly on June 6 that he "brought home my shays, read & wrote." The new carriage is startling, for Rufus rarely wrote about buying anything. Purchasing an expensive carriage so soon after his mother's death may indicate that she had left him money or that, with his mother and grown children no longer needing his care, he had time to travel long distances in style and comfort.

The year 1810 showed Rufus's proximity to changes coming to the Farmington Valley. In August, he visited a nearby textile manufactory, where a carding machine made rolls of cotton or wool that would be spun into thread. He seemed transfixed by what he was seeing, writing how he "went to the carding machine…tarried long at the mashine waiting for roles." It is likely this manufactory was in Farmington, as by 1816 the town had six carding mills.

Tourists were also coming near Northington to see the new observation tower erected this year atop Talcott Mountain, the first of four towers preceding today's Heublein Tower. Daniel Wadsworth, Hartford's wealthiest citizen, opened part of his 250-acre Monte Video estate and summer home to visitors, and his fifty-five-foot-high tower offered panoramic views of Hartford and the Farmington Valley.

Changes came also in the mission field, as more areas opened up to settlers. On September 5, 1810, a fair and hot Wednesday, five delegates from Connecticut and Massachusetts met at Reverend Noah Porter's home in Farmington and founded the first foreign missionary society in the United States: the American Board of Commissioners for Foreign Missions. Connecticut governor John Treadwell, Rufus's Yale classmate, was elected president, and the commissioners would soon send ministers to Native American tribes in the American West and to India and Burma. In time, the organization would become the United States' leading mission organization, known today as Global Ministries. Rufus's friend Dr. Solomon Everest became a major supporter of the American Board and established the Everest Fund with a bequest of $1,000 at his death in 1822.

Marriage and census records of 1810 reveal family news that fall. Zerah Hawley, a dentist and apothecary in New Haven, married Harriet Sherman on October 18. In Northington, the 1810 federal census listed the two Rufus Hawleys one after the other, indicating that Rufus Forward Hawley, with his wife, Betsey, and their five children, were living either next door to Reverend Rufus and Elizabeth or sharing the big parsonage. With those two kitchens in the pastor's house, it is likely that both Hawley families were living together. The New Year's Eve entry in the journal is once again extremely dark:

> *The year rolls round, & Steals away*
> *the breath yt first it gave;*
> *whate'er we do, whate'er we be,*
> *we're travailling to the grave.*

1811

June 24 Monday fair extreme hot & dusty. Rode wt Mrs Hawley to Mr Robbins; Norfolk.

June 27 Thursday Raind most of the day. We rode through Albany and Shenactady. we were robed of our trunk; but recovered it again.

Turning seventy years old in February, Rufus Hawley was strong enough to spend a day visiting almost every house on Lovely Street. Although young men chopped his wood, he could still do his chores in the snow. He was also vigorous enough to undertake a roundtrip journey of more than one thousand miles, traveling for what appears to be the second time to Ohio.

On June 27, Rufus and Elizabeth left on a three-month trip to the Western Reserve to see his sons Timothy and Jesse and her sons Gideon Curtis and Solomon Curtis. Four days from Northington, near Schenectady, Rufus caught a thief stealing his trunk from their new carriage from Hartford and called out, "Drop it, you scoundrel, or I'll fire!" The thief left the bags, but Rufus was completely undone by his lie; he had a whip to crack but no gun to fire. After later reporting this lie to the Hartford North ministers' association, he was told that the incident did not warrant further action.

Rufus and Elizabeth continued west through New York and Pennsylvania and into Ohio, where he preached at least thirteen times in meetinghouses, schoolhouses and homes. The pastor and his wife must have had a warm welcome, at least in some places. At this time, according to a letter by his son Timothy in 1808, the people in Ashtabula County, Ohio, heard preaching only about four times a year and were a "destitute [and] needy people."

Along the route, Rufus and Elizabeth stopped in more than fifty villages or towns, seeing friends and family and finding hospitality and entertainment. Upon returning home to Northington in September, Rufus learned of the death of Rufus Forward Hawley's daughter Maria, age four. The journal's last lines were about constant loss:

The present moments just appear,
Then Slide away in haste,
That we can never Say, they're here
But only Say, they're past.

11

WE SPEND OUR YEARS

Meetinghouse Mayhem, 1812–1816

1812

SEPTEMBER *16 Wednesday fair & very pleasant. Wrote, visited wt Mrs Hawley at Mr Danl Wadsworth's & read.*

DECEMBER *31 Thursday cloudy, but moderate. Studied, wrote, & married Calvin Allyn of Simsbury & Elisabeth N. Wilcox of Northington.*

Reverend Justus Forward semi-retired this year in Belchertown, perhaps putting in sharp focus for his Northington cousin that other endings were on the horizon. Rufus was glad for the help of "young men who gave me a spell cuting & piling wood at the house" but did not complain about getting out of bed one night to pray and talk with Mercy Northway. He enjoyed a visit with his wife, Elizabeth, to Daniel Wadsworth's observation tower on Talcott Mountain.

National and personal events weighed heavily on Rufus and others. In June, the United States declared war on Great Britain. Justus Forward wrote in his journal on December 31, 1812, that "the world is in a tumult. Europe is involved in bloody wars." For Rufus and Elizabeth, the departures of Hawley family members must have been hard to bear. Zerah and Minnie, with their toddler Edward Eugene, moved to New York. On September 2, the active and strong Rufus Forward Hawley (who also had a hasty and harsh temper) left for Ohio with Amon Hawley, along with a Mrs. Waters and her son.

But there was also happiness in the family. On October 29, on a day the pastor spent gathering apples, his son Rufus Forward returned from "Newconnecticut." He brought with him his niece Sophia, age seventeen, Timothy's daughter, and undoubtedly news from Austinburg. Dr. Orestes Hawley had raised enough money to replace the log meetinghouse with a New England–style structure and to top it with the first steeple on the Western Reserve.

In October, at the monthly meeting of ministers, Rufus, now seventy-one, agreed to help write a paper on the meaning of the covenants, and he wrote in the journal of a routine daytrip to Hartford for a missionary meeting. Traveling over Talcott Mountain to Hartford must have seemed an easy trip compared to the round-trip journey to Ohio.

But the time had come to stop writing. On this year's final Sunday, December 28, Rufus preached in the frigid and dilapidated meetinghouse from the Book of Isaiah, chapter 40. It is unclear which verse he spoke on, but it is perhaps fitting that the words of the first verse of the chapter are what he always strived to do: "Comfort my people."

On Thursday, December 31, 1812, Rufus Hawley performed the marriage of Elisabeth Wilcox and Calvin Allyn. The journals end that day, completing a remarkable run of fifty years. Perhaps he knew this would be his last entry, with vision failing, hands trembling and fire dwindling.

Reverend Rufus Hawley's final entry in his journal, December 31, 1812, after writing for fifty years: "We spend our years as a tale that is told." *Hawley-August Collection, Avon Free Public Library. Photograph by John Pecora.*

As Reverend Rufus Hawley wrote his customary New Year's Eve lines, the carefully chosen words seemed to be from a man utterly finished with accounting for every one of his days and years. That night, he left the story of his life to his family and to the ages: "We spend our years as a tale that is told."

1813–1816

The journals were finished, but there was more to the story of Reverend Rufus Hawley. Turning seventy-two years old in 1813, he kept his horse shod and his carriage repaired, paying blacksmith Isaiah North with beef. Of his six sons, only Rufus Forward Hawley lived in Northington. Zerah was in New Haven and Washington in Eldridge, New York; the other three sons lived in Ohio (Jesse in Morgan, Orestes in Austinburg and Timothy in Jefferson).

Yale Professor Benjamin Silliman, in his *Remarks Made on a Short Tour Between Hartford and Quebec in the Autumn of 1819*, described Northington about this time, with details that Rufus Hawley never recorded:

I once attended public worship there on a pleasant but warm summer sabbath. The house was almost embowered in ancient forest trees; it was smaller than many private dwelling houses; was much dilapidated by time, which had furrowed the gray, unpainted shingles and clapboards with many water-worn channels, and it seemed as if it would soon fall. It was an interesting remnant of primeval New England manners. The people, evidently agricultural, had scarcely departed either in their dress or their manners, from the simplicity of early rural habits. I do not mean that there were no exceptions, but this was the general aspect of the congregation; and, from the smallness of the house, although there were pews, it seemed rather a domestic than a public religious meeting.

The appearance of the minister [Rev. Rufus Hawley], was correspondent, to that of the house and congregation, as far as antiquity and primeval simplicity were concerned, but he was highly respectable for understanding, and sustained, even in these humble circumstances, the dignity of his station.

He was an old man with hoary locks, and a venerable aspect, a man of God of other times [emphasis by Silliman],— *a patriarchal teacher—not caring for much balanced nicety of phrase, but giving his flock wholesome food, in sound doctrine and plain speech. His prayers had that detail of petition, that specific application, both to public and private*

Benjamin Silliman (1779–1864), Yale College (1796) and one of Yale's first professors of the sciences. Silliman described Northington's meetinghouse and people in his *Remarks Made on a Short Tour Between Hartford and Quebec in the Autumn of 1819.* Collection of the Connecticut Historical Society, Hartford, Connecticut.

concerns, and that directness of allusion to the momentous political events of the day, and their apparent bearing upon his people, which was common among our ancestors, and especially among the first ministers who brought with them the fervor of the times when they emigrated from England.

Rufus Hawley was "of other times," as Professor Silliman noticed. His shabby meetinghouse was in a ridiculously inconvenient location, most of his good friends were gone and his parish's population was too widely dispersed. All signs pointed to a once-respected and beleaguered eighteenth-century pastor on the verge of forced retirement. Several decades later, Reverend Stephen Hubbell of Avon described the conflict over where to build a new meetinghouse as "rocking through the parish life like an earthquake."

There had been attempts to maintain the meetinghouse and pastor. Rufus still received his annual salary ($200) and twenty cords of free wood, and the meetinghouse windows had been fixed in 1806 and 1809. There were other meetinghouse repairs in 1813, the same year the Bridge Building Committee billed Farmington for building the "Northington meeting house Bridge." Ebenezer Miller swept the meetinghouse clean once a month, and in 1814, according to custom, the meetinghouse seating arrangement was reshuffled.

But circumstances continued to unravel for the pastor. In March 1814, he suffered two grievous blows when his brother Thomas Hawley and cousin Reverend Justus Forward died within a span of two weeks. Reverend Forward had also been a one-parish pastor, and his epitaph, almost illegible today on his gravestone in Belchertown's South Cemetery, could easily apply to his steady and beloved Northington cousin:

> *Sacred to the memory of Rev. Justus Forward, pastor of the church in Belchertown, who, skilled in Evangelical Doctrine, exemplary in Christian duty, prudent in council, valiant for the truth, faithful and, successful in labours, after a long and useful ministry, in which with reputation to himself, and to the spiritual benefit of his flock, he served God, and his generation, fell asleep March 8, A.D. 1814, in the 84th year of his age, and, the 59th of his ministry. Blessed are the dead who die in the Lord.*

By 1816, Northington clearly needed a new pastor. At the society meeting in June, those present agreed that Rufus Hawley could keep the 150-pound settlement he had received long ago in 1769. However, as he was informed shortly by a committee of five, he must have a colleague settle with him or resign.

12

SOME FRIENDLY HANDS

Catch'd on Fire, 1817–1819

R everend Rufus Hawley had four conditions for retiring or accepting a colleague as a co-pastor, and all four related to how much money he should be paid by the society. On November 10, 1817, after the society refused them all, the pastor offered one more idea, and the society agreed. As soon as the society found others to "supply the pulpit," Rufus would receive his overdue salary of 150 pounds and fifteen cords of free wood and give up claims to any future payment.

Filling the pulpit after this date were pastoral candidates and church members. A month later, on December 11, 1817, Rufus agreed in writing to relinquish "all further demands upon the society." Rufus's pastorate was finished. His son Rufus Forward delivered his father's last free wood.

Reverend Hawley's settled pastorate had officially lasted forty-eight years, from December 7, 1769, when he was ordained, until his written resignation on December 11, 1817. From this time on, for six more years until January 1824, he occasionally officiated and took part in ceremonies. The exact length of the pastorate, however, varies depending on the criteria. A fifty-seven-year pastorate counts the year he preached as a candidate (beginning December 4, 1768) and includes the pastor emeritus status he seemed to carry for the final eight years of his life. The West Avon Congregational Church counts his pastorate as fifty-one years, from ordination in 1769 until 1820, when Reverend Ludovicus Robbins became pastor.

Life in Northington changed dramatically that December 1817, and not only because the pastor resigned. For the past two years, emotions in the society had seemed to be on fire with divisive attempts to choose a central place for a new meetinghouse. Votes had come and gone since 1808 as potential locations were identified and staked. Even when the Connecticut General Assembly chose a new site at the parish's request, the parish rejected the proposal.

On a day or night less than a month after Rufus Hawley resigned, and sometime between the society's December 18, 1817, meeting and the morning of December 31, the meetinghouse burned down clear to the ground. A description of the meetinghouse by Serepta Gillette, thirteen years old at the time, appeared in the *Connecticut Courant* in 1919. The drafty meetinghouse, she said, rested on open foundations, and sheep took shelter under it during storms. She detested the cold meetings in what she called "the Lord's Barn," was "glad" when it burned down and "well remembered the whipping her mother gave her" for saying so.

The fire was no accident. West Avon Congregational Church pastor Reverend Joel Grant, in his centennial sermon about thirty years later, said that "the fire was considered the work of an incendiary, though a poet's imagination might fairly represent that the house itself, conscious that every beam and pillar in it was sacred, and that, instead of being a dwelling place for the prince of peace, it had become an arena for angry combatants, invoked some friendly hand to apply the torch, choosing to perish rather than suffer further desecration."

Burning of the first meetinghouse in Northington (today Avon) in December 1817. One of ten paintings by Janice Loeffler (1924–2009), illustrating "Avon Connecticut" by Mary-Frances Mackie, published in 1988. *Collection of the West Avon Congregational Church; used also with permission of the Avon Historical Society. Wick Mallory Photograph, 2011.*

Was Reverend Hawley the friendly hand who set the fire? Would a seventy-six-year-old man venture out on a winter's day or night to destroy the meetinghouse that symbolized his life's work? Certainly, no one would have thought it unusual to see him near the meetinghouse at an odd hour. With his strict conscience, however, it is unlikely he could have justified such an act, even if it was to finish off a hopeless building causing so much discord. The mystery of who set the fire remains, and the list of suspects includes the pastor, furious parish residents and mischievous children with hot embers.

The only thing for sure was that it was arson. On December 31, 1817, the church minutes recorded that the society members gathered at Captain Silas Goff's house. The prudential committee, they decided, would advertise in a Hartford newspaper and offer a reward for "apprehending the person or persons that caused the meeting house to be burned in Northington." The committee voted that until there was a new meetinghouse, worship services would alternate between the Hawleys' home and the Center School House.

Parts of the meetinghouse were saved: the large stone doorsteps were moved to Reverend Rufus's house, and Obadiah Gillet sold the old nails and stones. Still up for grabs was the question of where to rebuild. The power and votes had shifted west with the development of Lovely Street and Whortleberry Hill and with adding part of Burlington to the parish. Residing in this western section of Northington and representative of its growing power were the fashionably dressed Romanta Woodruff and his wife, Hannah. Samuel Broadbent painted their portraits in 1819, the earliest images of Northington residents, and Romanta proudly wrote of the portrait in his diary: "Doc't Broadbent here taking my likeness."

The controversy about where to build a new meetinghouse had been swirling around the parish for ten years, and there had been about twenty votes taken on the subject at society meetings. The Northington Ecclesiastical Society's final vote on where to put the new meetinghouse of the Second Church of Farmington (today known as the West Avon Congregational Church) took place on March 2, 1818. The tally of forty-three votes to thirty-seven settled the question: it would go on Northington's west side near the Center School House. The chosen land was swampy, unfit for farming and just east of the new burying ground that had been established in 1798. The church minutes do not mention construction, recording only on November 9, 1818, that society meetings would be held in the future at the center schoolhouse or (when it was ready) at the new meetinghouse.

This new meetinghouse was half a solution to a crisis that had split the congregation and probably broke Rufus's spirit. Staying with the majority of voters, he would attend this church in West Avon one mile from his home,

Above: Romanta Woodruff (1787–1837) and his wife, Hannah Robbins Woodruff (1795–1864). Romanta Woodruff, distiller and farmer, holds a book titled *Agriculture*. The Woodruffs lived at what is today 45 Edwards Road, Avon. *Portraits by Samuel Broadbent, May, 1819. Oil on canvas. Collection of the Connecticut Historical Society, Hartford, Connecticut.*

Below: West Avon Congregational Church, 280 Country Club Road, built in 1818. On March 2, 1818, the Northington Ecclesiastical Society voted forty-three to thirty-seven to build the Second Church in Farmington, in Northington's geographic center. The church divided, and Reverend Hawley stayed with the majority that built this church that year. This view dates to before 1969, when the church was moved across Burnham Road. *Photograph copy by Wick Mallory, 2011. Collection of the West Avon Congregational Church.*

today at 280 Country Club Road. (In 1969, this meetinghouse was moved from the northeast corner of the Country Club Road and Burnham Road intersection to the northwest corner.)

Those thirty-seven dissenters established the Third Church in Farmington (also called the United Religious Association of Farmington) in 1818, at 6 West Main Street in Avon. Their meetinghouse, designed by architect David Hoadley and today on the National Register of Historic Places, was built in 1819 beside the Talcott Mountain Turnpike. The church's first pastor, Reverend Bela Kellogg, settled that year and stayed until 1830. Professor Benjamin Silliman admired the new structure, today called the Avon Congregational Church. "In the valley of Northington," he wrote in the fall of 1819, "we passed a beautiful new meetinghouse. It is a handsome specimen of architecture...recently erected in this little parish, which, a short time since, had only one miserable ruinous house, situated in the midst of a forest."

Martha Hubbell, the wife of Reverend Stephen Hubbell, the church's pastor from 1840 to 1853, wrote in her book *The Shady Side* that "the [Avon Congregational] church looks out at you, fair and grave, through its veil of leaves." She noted the "plain, simple manners of [Avon's] agricultural population" and delighted in the "beautiful panorama" looking west from the Avon Mountain road (today Route 44). "Descending through overhanging woods," wrote Mrs. Hubbell, "grand old forest trees, you pace slowly up the wide-curved street of our little town, resting in its redundant maple-shade."

Martha Hubbell and Benjamin Silliman both knew that the two new Congregational meetinghouses did not represent excessive holy fervor or wealth. Silliman wrote in his 1819 report about the two churches:

> *We are not, however, to infer that increased resources, nor additional zeal for religion has reared these edifices; it was the effect of local jealousies, as to the place where a new house should be built, and how often, in our New-England villages, do we see this circumstance produce the same result, adding to the beauty; but, perhaps, not always to the harmony and piety of the neighborhood. Their aged minister [Rufus Hawley] is still living, but since the destruction of his ancient [meeting] house, and the division of his people, he is without any particular charge; still, however, although oppressed with the infirmities of advanced life, he occasionally officiates in public.*

West Avon's church struggled to take hold. In September 1819, the society minutes recorded that Daniel Wadsworth, the foremost citizen of Hartford, had donated sixty dollars and that Reverend Rufus Hawley was to

Avon Congregational Church, 6 West Main Street. Postcard, circa 1908. This church was built in 1819 and was called the Third Church in Farmington. Designed by David Hoadley and on the National Register of Historic Places, horse sheds are visible at the left. Church member Ruth H. Beeman sent this postcard to Lamont Cullen of Hartford on March 18, 1908: "Here's where I go every Sunday don't you wish you could?" *Collection of the Avon Congregational Church.*

visit and thank him. Furthermore, Rufus was to say that if the Wadsworth family attended worship, they could sit where they pleased. It is unlikely that the Wadsworths were contemplating that opportunity. West Avon's new church was in trouble, with the church split, members resigning and income dropping. In 1818, the new Connecticut Constitution had disestablished the Congregational church, no longer requiring everyone in a parish to pay taxes to support the minister. With people attending Baptist, Episcopal and Quaker services, or none at all, societies could not depend on their traditional Congregational church income stream anymore.

The trauma that Northington residents were experiencing through arson and political firestorms indicates that Rufus Hawley felt the division of his church keenly. He was desolate that he had failed to keep the one church together. The vital records, however, show some of what had made up his intense daily life as pastor: 1,075 births, 296 marriages and 352 deaths; he had performed 811 baptisms in Northington and in twenty-nine other towns and parishes of Connecticut, Massachusetts, Vermont and Ohio. He had also admitted 240 people to church membership, and his church had grown from 58 members when he began in 1769 to about 175 families at his resignation. Even with the church divided, did he take comfort in knowing that this work had mattered after all? Was there any satisfaction in knowing that part of his legacy would be a fragile stack of tiny journals?

13

MR. HAWLEY ENTERTAINED US WELL

A Son's Regret, 1819–1826

D ecember 1819 marked the fiftieth anniversary of Rufus Hawley's call to be pastor, and his grandson Edward Eugene Hawley wrote of hearing him preach his half-century sermon. One can imagine Rufus in the pulpit of the West Avon Congregational Church, looking out at the congregation and recalling for an instant that nervous young man in 1768 giving his very first sermon.

Rufus Hawley wrote his will in 1820. Still participating in religious ceremonies that year, he was one of six ministers at the Ordination Council of his successor, the unfortunate Reverend Ludovicus Robbins. The new pastor lasted less than two years, as the church could not pay his salary. Of his short and disastrous pastorate, Reverend Robbins wrote that he had felt useless and a burden to the society.

In the fall of 1820, Rufus's son Zerah left for northeast Ohio. Using Orestes's home in Austinburg as his base, Zerah traveled through the Western Reserve for a year. Two years later, he published a book based on the letters he wrote to his brother (probably Rufus Forward Hawley in Northington) during this time: the *Journal of a Tour thru Connecticut, Massachusetts, New York, Pennsylvania, Ohio and One Year's Residence in New Connecticut.* Showing an honesty that must have made his father proud, Zerah wrote the book to show "a true and just account" of life in Ohio for those considering settling in the area. The region's developers, warned Zerah, broadcast only a positive view, not the accurate picture. Returning to Connecticut, Zerah wrote emphatically that Ohio was "a society to which I am not accustomed and in which I am unwilling to live."

In 1821, Rufus and Elizabeth Hawley traveled again to Ohio to see his sons and to hand deliver his will to a friend, Dr. Giles H. Cowles of Austinburg. His health was so precarious that some doubted his safe return home. Thomas Gleason, the husband of Elizabeth's daughter Betsey, wrote in July from Homer, New York, to his brother in Hartford that "Parson Hawley and wife left here last Monday for N. [New] Connecticut. He stayed here about 3 weeks—his health was very poor I think it very doubtful whether he ever gets back to Connecticut." Rufus left his will and a codicil in the care of Dr. Cowles, a friend from Farmington, colleague from Yale, and pastor of the church in Ashtabula County.

A new age in transportation in Northington began in 1822, when the Farmington Canal Company received its charter. Rufus, eighty-one years old at the time of the charter, did not live to see the launch of the first canalboat six years later. The new eighty-four-mile water highway would connect New Haven with Northampton, Massachusetts, and link the Connecticut Valley to the markets of Long Island Sound and beyond, until railroad tracks replaced the canal bed in 1848.

Northington's commercial life was advancing, but not its religious life. At the February 28, 1823 meeting of ministers in the parish, Reverend Thomas Robbins did not mention the presence of Rufus Hawley and wrote that "our meeting has become small." Notwithstanding that day's eight-degree cold, and what he called "very blustering," snow, Robbins's comment seemed directed at both attendance and the group's vitality. The church in West Avon was in such dire straits by June 1832 that it asked today's Avon Congregational Church to "reunite" and share a pastor. The church in East Avon said no.

In January 1824, the West Avon church leaders invited Reverend Hawley to sit at the ordaining council for the new pastor, Reverend Harvey Bushnell. If Rufus attended the event in mid-January, it was one of his final acts of public ministry. A few weeks after the ordination, on February 3, Rufus hosted twelve other ministers at his home for a two-day association meeting. There was important business that day: awarding a license to preach to Alpheus Ferry, an 1821 graduate of Williams College. Reverend Thomas Robbins wrote in his diary that the temperature was a numbing ten degrees and that "Old Mr. Hawley is quite feeble, but comfortable, and entertained us well."

A week later, Reverend Robbins was back in Northington for a council meeting to advise people who were still uncertain about which church to attend. Northington's division into two Congregational churches had left people in conflict, clearly. The plan was that those living on the west side must unite with

The Journals of Rufus Hawley, Avon, Connecticut

Right: headstone of Reverend Rufus Hawley and his second wife, Elizabeth. *Left:* large headstone of his son Zerah and members of Zerah's family. West Avon Cemetery, Avon, Connecticut. *Photograph by Peter Wright, 2010.*

Reverend Bushnell's West Avon church and that the West Avon church must make all feel welcome. The location was still inconvenient for some, so Reverend Bushnell and the council of ministers recommended that worship could be held alternately in the meetinghouse and in a private home. As part of the council meeting, Reverend Robbins preached a sermon to a "very attentive" audience on how people must try to get along. "I hope this Society to be increased and prospered," Robbins wrote in his diary on February 10.

A year later, on a hot Friday, July 1, 1825, Rufus's wife, Elizabeth, age seventy-one, died. Her son-in-law Thomas Gleason praised her as a "kind and affectionate friend" and was sorry that he and her daughter Betsey Curtis Gleason could not be present at her mother's death. Thomas then lambasted Elizabeth Hawley's stepson Rufus Forward Hawley for the "cold indifferent" manner in which he informed the family of her passing.

Infirm and bereft, and having lost his wife after twenty-six years of marriage, Rufus died in Northington on January 6, 1826, tended by Dr. Alfred Kellogg. About two weeks later, Timothy Hawley, in Jefferson, Ohio, received a letter with the "melancholy account of Fathers Death," along with an account by a Mr. Squires, "who has lately returned [here] from Connecticut."

Timothy, the eldest son, immediately sent a letter to his brother Dr. Zerah Hawley in New Haven, dated January 27, 1826. Confident that "from his [Rev. Rufus Hawley's] own words that he had not an anxiety to stay longer," Timothy was relieved "to hear that his exit was as easy and calm as I believe it was." Timothy had worried greatly about his father, hoping that "he might be made comfortable and that his life should not have been embittered as it has been." Said Timothy with regret, "Could I live as I ought to live with as strict regard for duty as I believe Father did I think that many hours might be better enjoyed by me than some have been."

14

Beloved Sons

The Property Must Be Sold, 1826

Timothy Hawley, the executor of his father's will, had an uncomfortable feeling about settling the estate. He wrote to Zerah in his letter of January 27, 1826, that he would attend to the will "as soon as possible" and that he hoped to return to Connecticut in the spring. He also hoped that "all things may be conducted in the best manner without any unnecessary harshness or hard feelings & right & justice take place—I shall write to Rufus [Rufus Forward Hawley, in Northington] to delay proceedings as much as possible until matters can be attended to in a suitable manner & shall require of him [Rufus Forward] a correct Inventory." The brothers knew that their father's estate would not be settled smoothly.

Reverend Rufus Hawley had directed in his will that he be "buried in a decent, Christian manner." Mourners soon gathered at the West Avon Cemetery, across the road from the church. A shroud purchased from Martin Cowles covered his body; Darius Sperry made the coffin, and Alanson Woodruff dug the grave. Reverend Harvey Bushnell, pastor of the West Avon Congregational Church, likely conducted the funeral service, and the church bell tolled. The inscription on the simple gravestone for Rufus and his wife, Elizabeth, is barely legible today: "Rev. Rufus Hawley Died Jan...Mrs. Elizabeth wife of Rev. Rufus Hawley."

Four days later, the *Connecticut Courant* listed the late pastor's death notice: "At Farmington, on the 5th instant, Rev. Rufus Hawley, 88." The newspaper had the date and his age wrong, but the *Religious Intelligencer* was correct a few weeks later: "At Farmington (Northington Society) on the 6th inst., the Rev. Rufus Hawley, aged 84—a man of exemplary piety."

The inventory of the Hawley estate, the one of such concern to Timothy Hawley, was taken six weeks after his father's death by appraisers Abraham Chidsey and Roger Woodford. It listed the south half of the house, worth $250, and seventy-five acres of land ($600 value). It appears that his son Rufus Forward owned the north half of the house. In the Hawley barn ($75 value) were a sleigh, side saddle, harness, saddle and saddlebags, along with a barrel of meat and a barrel of cider. The list of Reverend Rufus Hawley's clothing showed an old shirt and two woolen shirts, a vest, a pair of breeches, two handkerchiefs, a coat, woolen stockings and leather gloves. He had an old hat and a best hat, a "great coat," a cloth cloak and a long frock coat called a surtout.

Rufus had also owned two chests of drawers, six old woolen and linen shirts, four pillowcases, diaper curtains, three tablecloths and three towels. The inventory listed a small table and a dressing desk, a table with falling leaves and six black chairs. The kitchen contained a low chest, a dining table, six old chairs, two chairs with arms, a rocking chair, a writing table with an account book and spectacles. There were two large and small brass kettles, a skillet, a large slice and tongs, andirons, a water pail, a quart pitcher, a teakettle, a bake pan, a pewter tea pot, an earthenware coffee pot, a chopping knife, nine knives and forks, two silver spoons, two iron candlesticks, a large and small looking glass and $2.25 in cash.

The books in Rufus's personal library were mostly religious: a Scott's Bible and a small Bible; a New Testament; a concordance to the Bible; William Burkitt's *Expository*; a history book by Benjamin Trumbull; four volumes of the *Connecticut Magazine*; and volumes of sermons by Reverends John Smalley of Berlin, Nathan Strong of Hartford, Nathan Perkins of Hartford, Joseph Washburn of Farmington and Jonathan Edwards Jr. There were religious writings by a Mr. Foster and Mr. McClur, a variety of election sermons, two volumes of *Prophesies* by Newton, David Humphrey's *Anarchiad: A New England Poem* and Timothy Dwight's writings on psalms. There were publications by Rufus's cousin, Reverend Justus Forward, but the appraisers did not take time to list them by their titles.

An old trunk contained Elizabeth Hawley's clothing: one silk gown and one silk shawl and three old gowns, one made of flannel and one of gingham. The clothing also included one bombast gown, a woolen shirt, a flannel petticoat and a great coat. The sleeping chamber had a carpet, a warming pan, two beds and pillows, a white blanket, a striped blanket and two plaid blankets. There were three quilts: one of calico and another of a blue fabric and the red quilt that Elizabeth made after her 1798 marriage to Rufus.

The estate's value of $1,040 placed Reverend Rufus Hawley solidly in Northington's middle class, with the most valuable possessions his seventy-five acres of land in Avon, the south half of the house and the barn. His most expensive household item was his Scotts Bible, worth eleven dollars. The pastor's will instructed that Rufus Forward would inherit his father's buildings, and the remaining property would be divided among all of his "beloved sons."

Reverend Rufus had, as it turned out, considerable debts. Timothy claimed that he and three of his brothers had lent their father a total of $1,292. Consequently, the estate owed Timothy, Jesse and Orestes several hundred dollars each, and $743 to Rufus Forward Hawley. In addition, Reverend Rufus's estate owed a total of $16 to those men who had served him at the end: Dr. Kellogg, coffin maker Darius Sperry, gravedigger Alanson Woodruff, Farmington merchant Martin Cowles (for the burial shroud) and the person who tolled the church bells.

As the estate's insolvency became clear, Timothy Hawley became infuriated at his brother Rufus Forward. Timothy suspected him of charging the estate for boarding their father, Rufus, and stepmother, Elizabeth, so that he could claim the assets and represent the estate as insolvent. Writing from Ohio, Timothy raged in a letter to Zerah in New Haven that their brother Rufus was trying to "sweep the whole" and that he believed Rufus Forward's dishonesty had caused the estate's insolvency. Timothy closed his letter abruptly as he rushed to his "haying & harvest."

Betsey Curtis Gleason was also extremely upset with the handling of her stepfather's estate. Writing from her home in Homer, New York, she had asked Rufus Forward Hawley for some of her late mother's silver spoons, bedding and clothing and felt anxious when she received no reply.

Rufus Forward Hawley then joined in the frantic words flying between Connecticut, Ohio and New York. Zerah, in New Haven, was in the middle of the squabble. Rufus Forward complained to Zerah that he (Rufus Forward) had certainly not represented the estate as insolvent and that he was ashamed to have a "Brother [Timothy] capable of such manners." He wrote that his brothers had never loaned their father any money, and therefore the estate owed them nothing. "Father," he declared, "never received a cent." Rufus Forward also justified his claim on the estate by saying that their father's will did not compensate him for working for free for his father until he was twenty-three years old, and "at any rate the property must be sold to pay the debts."

The Farmington Probate Court authorized Rufus Forward Hawley to sell the seventy-five-acre estate. On December 13, 1826, West Avon

Congregational Church moderator Stanley Day, the highest bidder, paid $553 for the barn, the south half of the house and the land, which included the ten-acre meadow between the Farmington Canal and the Farmington River. Rufus Forward Hawley continued to live in the house, which he later completely owned, along with more land than his father ever had in his life.

15

A CONFUSED HEAP OF RECORDS

Reverend Hubbell's Speech and Avon, 1828–1851

R ufus Forward Hawley continued farming on the Hawley homestead at
a time when Northington had a new canal, completed in 1828, slicing
its way through the landscape just east of the house. The parish also had
a new status and a new name. On May 5, 1830, the Connecticut General
Assembly approved a petition for the parish to become a town, proclaiming
that Northington would be "incorporated into a district town by the name
of Avon." At the first town meeting on Monday, June 21, 1830, Avon's
voters met at the West Avon Congregational Church for the "purpose of
organizing the Town of Avon." Town meetings would alternate between the
two Congregational churches until a town hall was built in the 1890s.

The new town had 1,025 residents, and the Farmington Canal streamed
through the town's center, going under the Albany Turnpike (Route 44) and
passing by the Canal Warehouse, Francis Woodford's three-story hotel, Obadiah
Gillet's Tally Ho Tavern and Inn, the Avon Congregational Church and the
new Baptist Church. The West Avon Congregational Church was two and
a half miles west from this hub, and located throughout the town were four
blacksmiths, two carding machines, three sawmills, two wagon shops, a tailor, a
shoe shop, a turning mill, a fulling mill, a gristmill, a cider mill, three distilleries
and five one-room schoolhouses. A sampler from 1830, stitched this pivotal
year by Emily Miller of Avon, age eleven, survives in the collection of the Avon
Historical Society.

Reverend Rufus Hawley's old house became known as Avonside, its
landmark significance apparent in a hand-drawn 1829 map on which the

The sampler by Emily Miller (1819–1880), age eleven, dated July 22, 1830, the year the parish of Northington incorporated as the town of Avon. Emily Miller, the daughter of Joseph and Catherine Case Miller, married George Mills (1817–1890) on August 31, 1843. They lived in Canton and had seven children. *Collection of the Avon Historical Society. Photograph by MotoPhoto.*

"R.F. Hawley" House appears as one of only five buildings the mapmaker felt worth noting, along with the two Congregational churches, one Baptist church and the Marshall Tavern. John Warner Barber stood on Avon Mountain (also known as Talcott Mountain) shortly after this, sketching the view of Avon below and including it in his book on Connecticut towns.

In 1837, Rufus Forward Hawley sold Avonside and eighty-two and a half acres for $1,080 to his nephew (and Reverend Rufus's grandson) Edward Eugene Hawley, twenty-six, of New Haven. With the house's adjacent kitchens, each with a gigantic fireplace and bake oven, there was plenty of room for Edward and his wife, Mary, who would have eight children. Joining them within the next three years were Edward's parents, Zerah and Harriet Hawley, and their other son, Robert Augustus.

Zerah Hawley must have been glad for the opportunity to go home, leaving a failing dental practice in New Haven. It seems he had more affection for the house than did his older brothers, for in 1799 he may have helped his father, Reverend Rufus, in its construction. Upon returning to Avon, said Edward Eugene Hawley, Zerah "engaged in agriculture, which was what he delighted in." Zerah's son Robert helped operate the farm. An account book kept by the Woodruffs, blacksmiths in Avon, listed repair work for Zerah in 1844–46: tempering chisels and augers, shoeing horses and fixing a corn mill crank and wagon tire. Zerah paid the blacksmiths with bundles of straw, old

The Journals of Rufus Hawley, Avon, Connecticut

Left: John Warner Barber (1798–1885), frontispiece in his book, *Connecticut Historical Collections* (1836). Born in Windsor, Connecticut, he trained from 1814 to 1829 as an engraver's apprentice in the East Windsor shop of Abner Reed. Barber was an author, publisher and original printmaker. *Collection of the Connecticut Historical Society, Hartford, Connecticut.*

Below: John Warner Barber's "Eastern View of Avon," October 7, 1834, including the Baptist church in the center and the Avon Congregational Church spire. Between 1834 and 1836, Barber sketched 104 Connecticut towns, traveling in a horse and buggy between April and November. His diary recorded the exact day he drew his pencil sketches, which he made into wood engravings for his book, *Connecticut Historical Collections* (1836). *Collection of Nora Howard. Photograph by John Pecora.*

horseshoes and old iron and with cleaning teeth (valued at one dollar) and extracting teeth (valued at fifty cents a tooth).

In 1851, when Avon's two Congregational churches commemorated the West Avon Congregational Church's centennial, Reverend Stephen Hubbell, pastor of the Avon Congregational Church, gave the centennial address. His words contained clues about Reverend Rufus Hawley's declining health in the 1820s and about the preservation of the Hawley family papers. To prepare his historical address, Reverend Stephen Hubbell talked to those who remembered earlier days and introduced Zerah at the ceremony as "a representative of the old pastor's family."

With details that Zerah must have supplied about his father, Reverend Hubbell said that

> *sad was the sight which then presented itself to the view of the aged Pastor, who for nearly fifty years had led a united flock. Feeling the effects of age, and wearied by his ineffectual efforts to heal divisions which could not be healed, he consented to the ordination of a colleague to assist in his Pastoral duties. A large part of his flock was, however, scattered to other folds.*

Reverend Hubbell said that in preparing his remarks, he had found an alarming lack of historical information:

> *We now come to a chasm in the history of the church which we must bridge as best we can. The records kept by Mr. Hawley are among the missing materials greatly needed in preparing this sketch. Whither said records ran some six or eight years since, or in what confused heap of antiquated almanacs and rejected papers they have hid themselves, we have yet to learn.*

16

YOU HAVE TO GO

The Remarkable Journals in Kind Hands, 1856–2002

It is likely that Zerah's son Edward Eugene Hawley, age forty-nine, attended the centennial celebration of Avon's congregational churches in 1851. Reverend Stephen Hubbells's sharp suggestion in his centennial address that the Hawleys were not caring for the family papers may have stung, sparking Edward's passion for family history. Five years later, in 1856, when his father died, perhaps Edward felt even more urgency to preserve the family papers, and he also may have had more time and leeway to work with the collection.

Edward compiled biographical sketches of his father Zerah and his five uncles—Timothy, Jesse, Orestes, Rufus Forward and Washington. He wrote out selected passages from his grandfather's journals of 1763 to April 1807, making the words easier for others to read. His transcription, however, omitted entire sections, weather references and the scriptural passages his grandfather preached.

Edward Eugene Hawley perhaps spent too much time at his desk and not enough time farming, for by the spring of 1861 he was in financial ruin. The nation's crisis added to Edward Eugene's personal troubles: his son Eugene Fowler Hawley, age eighteen, felt trapped at home and begged his father to allow him to fight in the Civil War. These conversations were going on all over town, and the stakes could not have been higher. Based on the 1860 census count of 515 men in Avon, about 18 percent of the town's males would join the Union army. Of these 94 men, 2 died in battle and 23 more died of wounds, disease or accidents. Sixteen were disabled, 18 wounded and 15 became prisoners of war.

Edward Eugene Hawley (1811–1868) was the son of Dr. Zerah Hawley. Edward lived in the house of his grandfather, Reverend Rufus Hawley, transcribed some of his journals and recorded family history. *Hawley-August Collection, Avon Free Public Library.*

Eugene's father let him join up, admitting that "I fear to have you go, and yet I am desirous that you should go." Edward would have readily fought and died himself, writing, "I should have no objection to being shot in a good cause under my present sorrows, poverty, and indebtness, with all my plans blasted." Eugene Hawley fought in the war for three years, survived Confederate prisons and the Battle of Gettysburg and returned to Connecticut in 1864. His brother, and Reverend Hawley's grandson, Robert Augustus, died at Antietam, leaving six children.

When Edward Eugene Hawley died in 1868, his daughter Florence Genevieve Hawley inherited Avonside. Florence had grown up in the Hawley house but preferred living in Hartford. Avonside became her summer house, where her sisters Bertha, Eva and Eudora also gathered. Upon Florence's death in 1930, Bertha Hawley inherited Avonside. Four years later, at Bertha's death, her history-loving nephew (Reverend Rufus Hawley's great-great-grandson) Reginald Birney, an insurance executive, inherited the forlorn house.

Reginald and his wife, Grace Johnson Birney, lived in West Hartford, but family photographs and letters suggest that they had loved visiting Avonside and their Hawley aunts in the summertime. Photographs from the 1890s show the house from charming and artistic perspectives, with Reginald, Grace and the aunts enjoying one another's sometimes silly company. Passionate about his family's history, Reginald corresponded with Hawley descendants for over twenty years, collected genealogy and made family trees.

Top: Near the Reverend Rufus Hawley House, July 1897. Reginald Birney (1867–1936), great-great-grandson of Reverend Rufus Hawley and a Hartford insurance executive, inherited the house in 1934 from his aunt Bertha Hawley. Titled "Avonside, The road to the village," the photograph shows a woman walking on a section of Old Farms Road, between the house and Avon center. *Birney Photograph Album, Hawley-August Collection, Avon Free Public Library. Photograph copy by MotoPhoto.*

Bottom: "Avonside by Special Request," July 1897. On the grounds of the Reverend Rufus Hawley House, Grace Johnson Birney is directly above the man on the right. This photograph is an informal view of a set, all taken in that tree. The title, in quotation marks on this and other photographs in the Birney Photograph Album, was probably written by Reginald Birney. *Birney Photograph Album, Hawley-August Collection, Avon Free Public Library. Photograph copy by MotoPhoto.*

"Avonside—the parlor," August 1896. The Reverend Rufus Hawley House, Avon, Connecticut. A plant on a high shelf drapes down in the corner, and a paper fan is displayed above a small picture of a bird on a branch. *Birney Photograph Album, Hawley-August Collection, Avon Free Public Library. Photograph copy by MotoPhoto.*

When Reginald Birney died in 1936, the fate of Avonside was in the hands of Grace Birney. A fire in 1950 damaged the two kitchens and the wood paneling, destroyed the main stairway and broke her heart. Fortunately, the journals and other Hawley papers had descended through the family and were safe in her possession. When she decided to sell the Avon house out of the Hawley family for the first time in five generations, Grace wanted an appreciative buyer and a steward for the Hawley papers.

Robert and Gladys Thompson August had both grown up in Avon and felt that buying the Hawley house was an opportunity of a lifetime. To Grace Birney, selling the house was an ordeal. When she visited Avonside with the Augusts to show them the property boundaries, she could not bear to look at the house and covered her face when she got too close. The front door had been stolen, the house had been invaded by animals and scavengers and a

The Journals of Rufus Hawley, Avon, Connecticut

"Avon-In Love, Old Bridge Pier Looking South," August 1896. Reginald Birney (1867–1936), great-great-grandson of Reverend Hawley, and Grace Johnson Birney (1875–1963) beside the Farmington River; they were married in 1897. They are seated near the location of the bridge (no longer standing) connecting west Avon (near today's Country Club Road and Old Farms Road intersection) to the meetinghouse across the river. *Birney Photograph Album, Hawley-August Collection, Avon Free Public Library. Photograph copy by MotoPhoto.*

ladder led to the second floor. Later on, when the Augusts went to the attic, they found clothes and newspapers a foot deep on the floor. There seemed to be nothing left of historical interest.

After the Augusts purchased Avonside in 1951, they installed heat, electricity and water and performed other renovations to the structure, keeping as near as possible to the original. Soon, they learned that items of historical interest had indeed survived. One day, to their complete surprise, Grace Birney gave them the Hawley journals and family papers. Robert and Gladys August knew the historical value of what Grace had so trustingly given to them, and they took on the responsibility of preserving the extraordinary collection. They stored the journals in archival-safe materials; studied the Hawley family history; alphabetized the index of journal names; arranged the Civil War papers of Eugene Fowler Hawley and the family photographs; opened the collection to local historians Christopher Bickford, Mary-Frances MacKie and others; and became active members of the Avon Historical Society.

After Grace Birney's death in 1963, her daughter called the Augusts at Avonside and asked if they wanted an oil painting of the Hawley house by artist George E. Candee. Gladys August never saw her husband, Bob, move so fast as he did that morning when he rushed to fetch the painting.

The Augusts sold their home in 1998, after owning Avonside for almost fifty years, and took the Hawley archive collection with them to their new

"Avonside, Two in a Hammock," July 1897. Reginald and Grace Birney visited their Hawley aunts at the Reverend Rufus Hawley House during summers. *Birney Photograph Album, Hawley-August Collection, Avon Free Public Library. Photograph copy by MotoPhoto.*

"Avonside, Two Cranks," July 1897. Near the Reverend Rufus Hawley House. Grace Birney is at right. *Birney Photograph Album, Hawley-August Collection, Avon Free Public Library. Photograph copy by MotoPhoto.*

house in Avon. The new owners of the Hawley house, Mark and Courtney Robinson, are equally committed to preserving the house and its history.

In 2002, following the tradition of keeping the Hawley family archives in town, Bob and Gladys August donated the Hawley journals, letters, genealogies and photographs to the Marian Hunter History Room of the Avon Free Public Library. The circle was complete: the journals of Avon's Reverend Rufus Hawley would stay in Avon.

Avon today would be, for the most part, utterly unrecognizable to Rufus Hawley. Some things, however, would be familiar: the rushing Farmington River, the slopes of Avon Mountain, spring buds, the calls of birds in the quiet burying grounds, the taste of watermelon, a flapping fish on the line and a crackling fire.

What began as a community of farmers from Farmington is now a town of eighteen thousand residents. It is entirely possible that Rufus, a man who seemed generous of heart and had streaks of adventure and curiosity, would embrace Avon and marvel at its seven churches and six religious traditions: the Avon Congregational Church, the Church of St. Ann, Christ Episcopal Church, Memorial United Methodist Church of Avon, St. Matthew's Lutheran Church, the West Avon Congregational Church and Valley Community Baptist Church.

17

CLOSELY ON THE LINE OF MIRACLES

The Legacy of Rufus Hawley

Farmington historian Mabel Hurlburt's *Farmington Town Clerks and Their Times* describes Reverend Rufus Hawley as "a very able and worthy man." Increase Tarbox, editor of Reverend Thomas Robbins's 1886 *Diary*, called him "the venerable Rev. Rufus Hawley." Reverend Stephen Hubbell of the Avon Congregational Church, knowledgeable through his friendship with Zerah Hawley, said in 1851 that "he died as he had lived, a man full of faith."

A more tempered view is in the *Memorial History of Hartford County.* Author Matthew Bartlett had grown up in Avon, the son of Reverend John Bartlett, pastor of the West Avon Congregational Church from 1835 to 1847. Matthew Bartlett was also connected to the Hawley family through his sister Delia Bartlett's marriage to Rufus's grandson Orestes. Matthew Bartlett, who must have heard stories, wrote that he was "not a man of brilliant parts, but a useful minister."

Rufus would have surely agreed that his life had been useful. He nurtured his church through the American Revolution and the beginnings of the Westward Movement; he had been steadfast and stoic through epidemics, accidents and tragedy. He came to Northington as a young Yale graduate and built what would become the West Avon Congregational Church, the Avon Congregational Church and the Avon Free Public Library. His marriages to Deborah and then Elizabeth had been long and, by every indication, congenial. Rufus and Deborah's six sons led useful lives as farmers, a blacksmith, a physician and a dentist; Timothy, Rufus Forward and Orestes, in particular, had become community leaders.

Reverend Thomas Robbins
(1777–1856) graduated from
Yale College in 1796 and was
Reverend Rufus Hawley's
colleague. Robbins collected
books, sermons and other
items of Connecticut history
and was a founder and first
librarian of the Connecticut
Historical Society. From 1803
to 1806, Reverend Robbins
worked with the Connecticut
Missionary Society, organizing
churches on the Western
Reserve (Ohio). *Collection of
the Connecticut Historical Society,
Hartford, Connecticut.*

Reverend Rufus Hawley's life may also have inspired two of his grandsons to become ministers and Civil War chaplains: Zerah Kent Hawley (Yale, 1833) was pastor in Illinois, Iowa, Tennessee and Connecticut and also author of *Congregationalism & Methodism* (1846) and *Defense of Our Fathers of New England* (1847). Zerah Kent's brother Reverend James Hawley (Yale, 1840) was pastor in Illinois, Michigan and Connecticut.

Reverend Thomas Robbins, pastor of East Windsor and founder of the Connecticut Historical Society (1825), was particularly interested in making Reverend Rufus Hawley's legacy even more useful. In the summer of 1826, six months after his colleague's death, Reverend Robbins visited Avonside. He had been in the house many times, and he knew exactly what it contained. A rabid collector of Connecticut history, he was there to buy items for his personal collection, one that ultimately would go to the Connecticut Historical Society. On that damp July day, Reverend Robbins wrote in his diary how he "looked over the remains of old Mr Hawley" and paid $1.88 for "pamphlets." Had he known about the journals? Had Rufus Forward Hawley refused to sell?

The survival of Rufus Hawley's thirty-three small and fragile journals is stunning. The author of the *Hawley Record* genealogy, Elias Hawley, would have agreed. From firsthand experience gained by visiting towns to collect material for his 1890 book, he wrote that the preservation of New England's town and church records was "closely on the line of miracles."

The Journals of Rufus Hawley, Avon, Connecticut

The Reverend Rufus Hawley House, 281 Old Farms Road, looking north, by George Edward Candee (1837–1907), possibly circa 1865–70. This painting shows the Avon Congregational Church steeple, Farmington River and possibly Mary, Eva and Josephine, daughters of Edward Eugene and Mary Hawley (Reverend Hawley's great-granddaughters and the artist's cousins). Candee lived in New Haven and studied with George Henry Durrie. *Painting exhibited at Connecticut Historical Society in 1992. Private Collection. Photograph by John Pecora.*

One of the most salutary effects of the historical and genealogical revival is the action being taken towards the safe keeping of the public records...But the church records I have reason to think are as much exposed as ever, being in no safer place than under an elder's or deacon's arm, in the minister's hat, or in the cupboard over the oven.

Reverend Rufus Hawley may well have tucked his journals under his hat or stashed them in his cupboard. The journals that miraculously survived tell a unique tale that is deeply personal. Through his words, he opens a remarkable window to his life and to a long-lost Avon, letting a world he would barely recognize peek through.

Appendix A

THE CHILDREN OF REVEREND RUFUS AND

DEBORAH HAWLEY

The Hawleys' six sons were born in Northington. Edward Eugene Hawley's descriptions are in his family history, *The Heraldic, Historic and Genealogic Exposition of Hawley*, in the collection of the Avon Free Public Library.

GEORGE WASHINGTON HAWLEY (January 26, 1777–1850 or 1851), called Washington by his father in the journals, was the fourth son, baptized by his father on March 9, 1777, in the Northington meetinghouse. On October 14, 1804, he married his second cousin Roxana Hawley (October 29, 1777–October 23, 1807), daughter of Gad Hawley and Lydia Gillett Hawley of northeast Farmington. Their two children were George Washington and Julia Roxana. Washington's wife Roxana is buried in Morgan Township, Ashtabula County, Ohio. Her gravestone says "wife of Mayor George W. Hawley." Washington married Polly Whitman of Farmington in 1815.

The 1850 census records him as a laborer and farmer in Elbridge, Onondaga, New York, age seventy-three, with Olive, seventy-two. His death date is uncertain, but he seems to have died by the fall of 1851.

Edward Hawley described his uncle Washington as "5 feet 11 inches [tall], strong, active, but of a morose disposition. When a boy he would do his bird hunting without a gun, as his skill in throwing stones as a mark was remarkable, seldom failing of hitting the object aimed at. He served his time as an apprentice at the hatting business."

JESSE DUDLEY HAWLEY (December 7, 1774–September 26, 1851) was the third son, baptized on January 15, 1775, by his father in the meetinghouse. He was married on May 6, 1799, in Granville, Massachusetts to Lydia Root (January 20, 1780–August 14, 1808). Their three children were Orestes, Philema and Elvira. Jesse married Nancy Hall on May 14, 1809, in Granville.

Jesse was bound in 1791 to Gad Taylor of Suffield, Connecticut, to learn the blacksmith trade. He was there for parts of two years and also worked in Colebrook for another blacksmith. Jesse had his own blacksmith shop in Granville, Massachusetts, in 1798 and was still there in February 1800. By 1807, Jesse was in Morgan, Ohio. In early 1851, according to the West Avon Congregational Church's centennial history, Jesse was "hale and hearty" and "still resides upon his farm, in Western New York." Jesse also lived in Napoli, New York.

Edward Eugene Hawley described his uncle Jesse:

> *Jesse Dudley was a tall, burly man, massive in frame of well developed muscle, broad shouldered, deep chested and very round. He was not as nervously made as Rufus Forward, and was inferior to him in activity, but superior in strength. Few men could compete with him in wrestling. He was educated as a blacksmith by trade, and although a man of sound judgment, and a keen reasoner, yet he was quite illiterate. Of a genial disposition, and shrewd joker, and quick in Repartee, he made himself agreeably companionable to his friends and acquaintances, and particularly to young children. He settled in the town of Morgan, Ashtabula County, Ohio, where as owning a large farm, and tavern stand he brought up his family, but a few years before he died he removed to Chatauqua County in New York State. He made several visits to the Eastern states in the course of his life, and was an efficient agent in procuring aid for Religious institutions in Ohio.*

DR. ORESTES KENT HAWLEY (September 16, 1778–March 21 1847) was the fifth son, baptized on October 25, 1778, by his father in the Northington meetinghouse.

As a child, Orestes attended an academy in Salmon Brook, Connecticut, taught school in New Hartford and Southington and studied medicine with Dr. Woodbridge of Southampton, Massachusetts, and with Dr. Everest. In 1799–1800, Orestes took a five-month trip noted in Rufus Hawley's journal as "to ye westward." Returning to Northington, Orestes married his cousin Ursula Hawley (1781–1803) on April 6, 1800; she was the daughter of Gad and Lydia Hawley of Farmington.

APPENDIX A

After recovering from smallpox, Orestes went again to New Connecticut in May 1800 and was the first physician in Ashtabula County. Orestes returned to Northington in September but left again for Ohio on February 16, 1802. His wife, Ursula, and child joined him there shortly, brought by his brother Timothy. Reverend Rufus Hawley received a letter reporting their safe arrival. "Praised be the Lord," he wrote in his journal on August 2, 1802.

Edward Eugene Hawley wrote about Orestes and Ursula's daughter Cybelia (and his cousin):

> *Of a lively disposition, and jovial humor, she took life easy, and seldom troubled herself to look for the shady side of any thing...She had not the sensitive delicacy of thought and feeling, which characterized her sister Eliza...was brought by her father* [Orestes Kent Hawley] *to Connecticut to finish her education, and for some time boarded with her Uncle Zerah in New Haven.* [She was] *graceful, accomplished, highly intellectual, with an engaging modesty of demeanor.*

After Ursula Hawley's death in 1803, Orestes had married Betsey Austin of Austinburg, Ohio, on July 24, 1804; she was the daughter of Judge Eliphalet Austin, one of the first settlers of Austinburg, a town in Ashtabula County, south of Lake Erie in the Connecticut Reserve of northeastern Ohio. Two-thirds of the county's settlers were from Connecticut. Orestes quickly became a community leader, working as county commissioner (1812–15) and treasurer (1815–18). Orestes and three other men helped raise the funds to replace the log meetinghouse with a New England–style structure. The new church, with the first steeple on Western Reserve, held its first service in 1815. Orestes and three other men helped raise the funds, holding the first service in 1815 in a church with the first steeple in the Western Reserve. By this time, Orestes was practicing medicine and was called "Doctor."

In 1831, Orestes Hawley was one of ten men who tried to establish the Ashtabula County Institute of Science and Industry, a school to train young men for the ministry. The institute was to be built in Mechanicsville, beside the Grand River, on the property of and near the gristmill, sawmill and oil mill of Hawley and fellow incorporator Joab Austin. The students would work on the land and in the mills. The founders abandoned this plan for financial reasons. In 1835, the school was renamed the Grand River Institute, and in 1840, with a broader curriculum, it began admitting women.

Orestes was a founder and vice-president of the newly formed Ashtabula County Female Anti-Slavery Society, of which his friend Betsey Cowles was another founder. In 1836, he was the Ashtabula County representative to the Ohio Anti-Slavery Convention and served as the manager of the resolution stating, "Resolved, That the American slave trade involves within itself all the cruelties and horrors of the African: therefore, we call on all those who are carrying it on, at once to cease."

Orestes's third wife, Polly Coe Hawley (1800–1877), was born in Hartland, Connecticut. Harriet Taylor Upton, in *The History of the Western Reserve*, described her as one of its "most ardent opponents of slavery" and said that "the Hawleys established at their house one of the most enterprising 'underground railway stations' in the region, often feeding, clothing and harboring men of the colored race while escaping to Canada." Polly's sons, Henry and Albert, who would have been very young children at the time of the 1836 convention, helped in the kitchen and harnessed up the horses to transport the fugitives. Polly hid fugitives under her haystack, including a woman named Clark. Polly Hawley, according to Upton, was Harriet Beecher Stowe's inspiration for her character Harris in *Uncle Tom's Cabin* (a claim that the Harriet Beecher Stowe Center, in e-mails to me in 2010, could not verify). At age eighty-seven, Polly Hawley received one of two hundred plates presented to American antislavery leaders by the English Anti-Slavery Society. Orestes is buried in Austinburg, Ohio, in a private cemetery in back of the former Austin-Ellsworth House.

Edward Eugene Hawley described his uncle Orestes:

> *Orestes Kent was a wonderful, stout, and robust man. He was the strongest of this strong family, and would throw around Jesse as an ordinary man would an infant. He had an enormous muscular development, and was in height and personal appearance very much like Jesse D. but his humeral muscles were so large as to give him a slightly stooping appearance. Hair dark brown, eyes grey, cold and calculating. He was educated a Physician and Surgeon, and settled in Austinburg, Ashtabula County, Ohio, where in the county he was preeminent in his profession, and by his untiring application, determined resolution, and close dealing, he accumulated a large property in real estate. As a physician in collecting his dues he was not forbearing, but would exact of the poorest of his patients their last cow or sheep; but he obtained credit in the benevolent, and charitable reports of the day, as a man of great liberality. There by this means he could obtain famous notoriety he gave by the thousand. But his wealth which he accumulated he could not bequeath to his posterity, as all died unmarried but Cybelia, who married St. John. He was prominent, and active, and influencial in many of the Religious and*

educational movements of this time. A man of strictly temperate principles and habits; and a downright and hearty hater of slavery.

RUFUS FORWARD HAWLEY (April 27, 1773–December 9, 1847) was the second son, baptized by his father on May 30, 1773, in the Northington meetinghouse. Rufus Forward taught school in West Hartford, Kensington, New Hartford and Norfolk. With Amasa Woodford, he set the town lines between Avon and Windsor and between Avon and Hartford.

Rufus married Betsey Richards (1776–1854) of Farmington on September 24, 1795. Rufus and Betsey, and their daughter Maria Evelina, joined the Avon Congregational Church on November 27, 1831. The church dismissed them on August 3, 1837, upon their move to Augusta, Illinois. Rufus and Betsey had twelve children.

Edward Eugene Hawley described his uncle:

Rufus Forward was a tall spair [sic] man, with large aquiline nose (characteristic of the family) light complexion, strong, nervous, active, with extraordinary powers of endurance. Eyes of light blue—hasty and harsh in temper—He resided on the family homestead until he was an old man, and then removed to [Augusta,] Morgan Co., Illinois, as he had children living there. He made one or two visits to Connecticut while he lived in Illinois. He was an energetic farmer both in Connecticut and in Illinois, and acquired a handsome estate. He was ardent, and thorough in his sentiments, particularly in his political views, being a thorough going advocate of temperance, and an ardent Antimason. He was a professing member of the Congregational church. He assisted in building the first church of the West Society, in the town (now of Avon) of Farmington, Parish of Northington. In this parish he brought up his family.

SOPHIA HAWLEY (November 18, 1782–December 11, 1784) was Reverend Rufus and Deborah Hawley's seventh child and only daughter; she may have been adopted. Rufus baptized her in the Northington meetinghouse on January 5, 1783. She died at age two after being scalded.

TIMOTHY RUGGLES HAWLEY (June 29, 1771–July 24, 1828) was Rufus and Deborah Hawley's first child, baptized on August 4, 1771, by his father in the Northington meetinghouse. He married Deborah Ingham (1770–July 7, 1851) of Northington on October 3, 1790, the daughter of Elizabeth Chalker and Jonathan Ingham. They had ten children.

The Ruggles name comes from Timothy's maternal ancestor John Ruggles, who arrived from London in 1635. Rufus's journal records that in 1787 Timothy taught school in Turkey Hills, Farmington, New Hartford and Northington. He also taught at Northington's Lovely Street School in 1789, 1791 and 1792. Timothy moved with his family from the east side to the west side of the Farmington river on March 20, 1792.

Timothy helped his father organize the Northington subscription library and served as treasurer of West Avon's Third School District, which stood from 1777 to 1799 on what is today the site of the West Avon Congregational Church. A second schoolhouse stood there until it was struck by lightning (1799–1822); the third schoolhouse (today the museum at 6 West Main Street) was then built near today's Avon Free Public Library.

Timothy's brother Orestes was already settled in northeastern Ohio when, in the spring of 1801, Timothy went there to plan for his own move. Working for the Torringford Land Company of Connecticut, Timothy surveyed and laid out Morgan Township. In return, he was granted a parcel of land. He went back briefly to Connecticut in the fall of 1801. The following March, in 1802, he returned with his wife, Deborah, and their oldest children (Sophia, Thales and Almon) to settle. Reverend Rufus wrote in his journal for April 12, 1802, that "Timothy, & his family, Chauncey Hawley, wt Orestes's wife & child set out for Newconnecticut."

When Timothy returned to Ohio this time, he brought with him Orestes's wife and child from Northington. Timothy and his family settled on his farm in Morgan, staying until 1811. After Timothy became county clerk for the newly created Ashtabula County, they moved to the county seat of Jefferson, where Timothy established a tavern. Timothy and Deborah are buried in Oakdale Cemetery in Jefferson, Ohio.

Edward Eugene Hawley described his uncle Timothy:

> *He was a tall, stout, and handsome man. Remarkably active and of a cheerful disposition. He lived and died in the faith of Christ. Exemplary in his conduct, and of irreproachable integrity. He was educated a land surveyor, and in his young manhood surveyed Canandaigua in N.Y. besides many tracts in N.Y and Ohio, contracting by exposure a disorder which shortened his life. He could have bought the whole site of Canandaigua for 25 cents per acre. His complexion was fair, light brown hair, blue eyes, and rosy cheeks.*

Dr. Zerah Hawley (April 14, 1781–March 6, 1856) was the sixth and youngest son of Reverend Rufus and Deborah Hawley. His father baptized him June 3, 1781, in the Northington meetinghouse. Zerah was the last surviving sibling. Married to Harriet "Minnie" Sherman (1788–1863) of New Haven on October 18, 1810, he returned after his father's death to live in the Hawley house in Avon.

Zerah and Minnie had six children: Edward Eugene (b. October 14, 1811; d. 1868); William Sherman (b. 1813; d. young); Harriet Amelia (1814–1897); Sarah Ann (d. by 1821); Robert Augustus (b. 1819; d. September 1862 at Civil War Battle of Antietam); and William Sherman (possibly d. August 30, 1824, in New Haven).

When Zerah was young, Farmington pastor Reverend Joseph Washburn tutored him for two years before he entered Yale in 1799. He graduated in 1803 and received his master's degree from Yale in 1808. Zerah wrote the *Journal of a Tour Through Connecticut, Massachusetts, New York, Pennsylvania and Ohio* (1822). He was a dentist and had an apothecary in New Haven (1810); he also relocated several times, practicing dentistry in New York (1812–16), Ohio (1816–21), New Haven (1821) and Avon. Zerah is the only one of Rufus and Deborah Hawley's children buried in the West Avon Cemetery. His remains are beside his father and stepmother, Elizabeth.

Edward Eugene Hawley described his father, Zerah:

In his boyhood was small, and not robust. Was fitted for college, and graduated with honor at Yale. On attaining to manhood the native vigor of his race developed itself in his person. His stature was 5 feet 11 inches, and well proportioned, with a spare muscular development, but active, and of nervous [illegible]. *He also could be classed with <u>strong men</u>. Complexion fair—a fair blue eye. Rather deep seated, beneath a short and thick eyebrow. Hair dark brown, and at thirty years of age slightly streaked with grey. On leaving college taught school in E. Windsor a short time, and then went to the Eastern shore of Maryland where he taught a high school for three years with great success. Returned to New Haven and studied medicine, and commenced business as apothecary and chemist in New Haven, Ct. in Chapel St. opposite the college. When first married lived in the old Presidents house in York St., where his first three children were born. Failed in business at the close of the war of 1812, and removed to New York, leaving his family in New Haven at the N.E. corner of York and Chapel Streets. Began business as a dentist in New York, and shortly brought down his family. Resided there four years, his health failed by reason of the bad water of the city, when he was induced by the Representatives of his brothers in Ohio to emigrate to their locality, where for one year he practiced* *medicine; had much sickness in his family, buried Sarah and discouraged, returned to New Haven in 1821 where he resumed in straitened pecuniary circumstances the business of dentistry, and continued in the same until 1836 or 7, when he removed to his fathers old homestead in Avon, and engaged in agriculture (which was what he delighted in) and continued in the same for the remainder of his life. He died on 6th March 1856 of paralysis from ossification of the ventricles, or arteries of the heart, after an illness of 53 hours, and was buried in the cemetery of the West Parish by the side of his father.*

PREHISTORIC FARMINGTON AND SETTLEMENT

Two hundred million years ago, dinosaurs roamed the Farmington Valley: Coelophysis, Anchisaurus and Eubrontes. Four million years ago, Lake Hitchcock covered Connecticut, and mountains as grand as the Alps arose. Time blew the mountains away bit by bit, and rivers carried their grainy pieces to the valleys. Over eons, this sediment hardened into sandstone and shale. Then came fiery lava and grinding earth, twisting into the steep cliffs of Talcott Mountain.

Glaciers came and went over the next two million years. Thick ice buried Connecticut at least four times, rubbing the rocks raw and leaving boulders from Vermont, New Hampshire and Massachusetts. It was enough to make a river go crazy. The Farmington River, which once flowed south, cranked into reverse and burst into the Connecticut River at Tariffville Gorge. After the ice melted twenty-five thousand years ago, hairy mastodons ten feet tall with massive trunks moved in.

About ten thousand years ago, River Indians settled the area, and by the mid-1600s, they were on the brink of being decimated by the Pequots to the south and the Mohawks to the west. They accepted the protection that the English presence promised, and the River Indian leader Sequassen sold the flat and fertile land that they called Tunxis to settlers from Hartford.

In 1645, the Connecticut General Assembly incorporated the River Indians's land as the town of Farmington. It measured over two hundred square miles, with its village on the eastern side, and some of the English settlers traveled up to twelve miles to reach their meetinghouse or to vote.

One of Farmington's founders was Stephen Hart, born in Essex, England, in 1605, with a bleak future of food shortages, a dying textile industry and limited land ownership. Hart helped establish the Farmington church and operated a mill, and his fifteen-acre home lot was four times bigger than anyone else's. About 1643, he acquired land three miles north of Farmington center, known afterward as "Hart's Nod." The term "Nod" came from the Tunxis word *noadt* for "far, far off" and also possibly from shortening "the North District" of Farmington.

Stephen Hart built a summer farmhouse (today 72 Cider Brook Road) and barn, and other Farmington families followed. What began as extra land for grazing and growing crops became a neighborhood. In 1750, this part of Farmington (the north part) became the parish of Northington. The name changed again in 1830, when it incorporated as the town of Avon.

THE NORTHINGTON MEETINGHOUSE

In the 1740s, when Rufus was a boy in Farmington, the land in the northern part of town was called Nod. About 160 people in thirty-one families lived in Nod and attended church about three or more miles away in Farmington. Nod's people soon required their own minister and convenient meetinghouse. So, in October 1746, the people of Nod petitioned the Connecticut General Assembly for permission to hire their own pastor for the winter months of December through March. With winter privileges, they could have religious services in a local home and would be exempt from paying Farmington society taxes. The General Assembly's granting of winter privileges was a temporary fix, however, that lasted four winters.

Nod's people soon judged themselves "ripe for being a society among themselves." In 1749, thirty-one men signed a petition to the Connecticut General Assembly, requesting that Nod be a separate ecclesiastical society, saying that they had "reason to hope, with the blessing of God on our labors, [that] we shall be well able to support the Gospel among ourselves for the future." In May 1750, the assembly granted their request to become the Farmington Second Society, also known as the Second Church in Farmington. Nod's new name was Northington (a contraction of North Farmington), a name that would last until 1830, when the parish incorporated as the Town of Avon.

By May 1751, Reverend Ebenezer Booge (Yale, 1748) had moved to Northington with his wife, Damaris Cook Booge. The little parish must have been thrilled that such a distinguished man accepted their call to settle as pastor. Reverend Booge, about age thirty-five and a joiner from East Haddam before graduating from Yale, must have been just as glad to finally have his own parish. The church was established that fall, on November 20, 1751.

Now that they had their own pastor, the people of Northington wanted a meetinghouse for Sunday religious services, society meetings and school exercises. Most Northington homes at this time were located east of the Farmington River, so the Hartford County Court directed that the new meetinghouse be situated there. Twenty-two inhabitants living west of the river signed a petition claiming hardship getting to the meetinghouse. They had a point, for until there was a bridge, they had to cross the river by horseback or canoe or use the bridge in Farmington four miles upriver.

With the court's decision, they put up a small and unfinished meetinghouse on the Farmington River's east side, on a half acre near the Nod path, at Barnabus Thomson's western boundary (the end of today's Reverknolls). It cost about 1,000 pounds, and its first worship service was on August 25, 1754. A new bridge linked the meetinghouse to the west side of the parish and lasted about ten years. This was the first of six bridges that were subsequently destroyed by ice and floods until 1828, when Farmington voted to discontinue "the old Northington bridge."

Church minutes, contemporary descriptions and the design of typical Connecticut meetinghouses give clues as to the appearance of Northington's meetinghouse in 1754. It was smaller than a typical dwelling house, probably plain and almost square, with its longer side and entry door facing the road. There was a large stone step at the west door and south door; it had clapboards (probably unpainted) and a bell tower. The high pulpit, with a cushion for the Bible, was opposite the main entry door, and there were simple box pews. The main door had a lock, and a man swept the meetinghouse clean once a month.

The second-floor seating gallery was left incomplete until seven years later, when taxes from nonresident landowners paid for finishing the first floor, building gallery stairs and laying an upstairs gallery floor. Three years after that, the society voted to finish the "fore part" of the meetinghouse. Taxes in the late 1700s paid for pine shingles, clapboards, nails, step stones, frequent window repairs and labor.

The pastor's family was seated near the pulpit, along with the prominent and the elite. There was a separate section for young men. Every few years, a committee decided the seating arrangement, assigning seats to families according to wealth, age and community status.

Reverend Booge taught some of the Northington boys Latin and Greek, giving them four months a year of free schooling at his home or in other houses and trying to prepare some of them for college. Also an author, in 1756 he published *The Unteachable, Forsaken of God*. He preached and administered the ordinances to his congregation and to neighboring parishes. Like the conservative mother-church in Farmington, he did not practice the 1662 Halfway Covenant of baptism, which was a liberal interpretation of baptism meant to increase the number of church members. In churches that followed the Halfway Covenant, if parents were not church members but had publicly declared their Christian faith and obedience, the pastor could baptize their child. In Reverend Booge's meetinghouse, however, a church member bringing a child for baptism had to be in full communion with the church and possess personal conversion experience.

The Halfway Covenant seemed to exasperate Reverend Booge. While on a pulpit exchange in West Simsbury in 1754, he wrote that Samuel Mills of West Simsbury was admitted to that church as a "half-member—I don't know what! May be a covenantee—for I think some call 'em so."

RELIGIOUS SERVICES IN THE

NORTHINGTON MEETINGHOUSE

Based on the Hawley Journals and Traditional Practices
of the Congregational Church

E very Sunday the Northington meetinghouse had morning and afternoon services lasting about three hours each. The solemn ceremony of communion, which Rufus called "administering the Sacrament," was held six times a year, on the first Sunday of the month every other month. To reenact the Last Supper, church members ate a bread morsel and took a sip of wine.

Baptisms and the acceptance of new members were held periodically in the meetinghouse. A typical Sunday morning and afternoon service each had opening prayer, a Scripture reading, a sermon, a main prayer and then psalm singing. The sermon lasted for one or one and a half hours, beginning with a reading from the Bible. Sometimes there was a collection for the needy. The closing blessing finished the service.

During the Sunday midday break of an hour and a half, the congregation ate, socialized and exchanged news. Rufus preached the afternoon's sermon on the same Bible passage as in the morning or on an entirely different passage.

Religious services were also held during the week, and these also followed the traditional Sunday order: services held for Fast Days, election days, Thanksgiving and the Friday Preparatory Lecture (held every two months before the Sacrament of the following Sunday).

THE TRUNK IS ALMOST STOLEN,

ALBANY, NEW YORK, 1811

When family historian and author Elias Hawley happened to meet up with Reverend S. Bartlett on a train in Hartford in 1847, Reverend Bartlett told him a story. Bartlett's niece, Julia Bartlett, had married Orestes Kent Hawley, Rufus Hawley's grandson, and she knew of a family tale:

> *It seems that some of the family of Rev. Rufus had emigrated to the West, and he wished to make them a visit. Taking his wife in his private carriage he started, having his trunk strapped on the rack behind. Having reached the then lonely sand plain covered with pines between Albany and Schenectady about dusk, and feeling somewhat insecure, he occasionally peered out between the curtains of the carriage-top to see if all was safe with the trunk.*
>
> *Once on looking he thought he discovered the trunk move but said nothing. Looking again it was gone. Quick as thought he threw the reins to his wife and leaped out and saw a robber dragging his trunk into the wood. Instantly raising his whip he exclaimed in a commanding tone: "Drop it, you scoundrel, or I'll fire." The frightened robber fled in marvelous haste, leaving the property which the owner took and went on his journey.*
>
> *But the incident left an unpleasant impression on the good man's mind. He conversed with his wife on the subject, and finally, on his return home, brought the matter before the Consociation as a case of conscience. He was far from being at ease because he had implied to the gentleman robber that he had fire-arms, when in fact he had nothing but a loaded whip.*

Appendix E

The Consociation, however, did not think he had very much exceeded the bounds of propriety in view of the short time he had to consider what course he should take or what language he should use, and passed the case as one on which action was quite unnecessary, and the Rev. Father was relieved of the burden on his conscience for having retained property by false pretense.

Towns of Baptisms and Towns of Guest Pastorates

From the West Avon Congregational Church Vital Records, with Name of Town Today

Towns of Baptisms

CONNECTICUT
Barkhamsted
Bristol
Burlington
Cambridge
Enfield
Farmingbury (Wolcott)
Farmington
Hartford
Harwinton
New Cambridge (Bristol)
New Hartford
Norfolk
North Windsor
Salmon Brook
Simsbury
Southington
Torringford (Torrington)
Turkey Hills (East Granby)
West Britain (Bristol)
West Hartland

West Simsbury (Canton)
West Suffield
Windsor
Winsted
Wintonbury (Bloomfield)
Worthington (Berlin)

MASSACHUSETTS
Milton
West Stockbridge

OHIO
Austinburg

VERMONT
Cornwall

TOWNS WHERE RUFUS HAWLEY WAS GUEST PASTOR

From His Journal Entries, with Name of Town Today

CONNECTICUT
Barkhamsted
Burlington
Cambridge
Enfield
Farmingbury (Wolcott)
Farmington
Hartford
Harwinton
New Britain
New Cambridge (Bristol)
New Hartford
Norfolk
North Branford
North Windsor

Poquonock (Windsor)
Salmon Brook (Granby)
Simsbury
Suffield
Torringford (Torrington)
Turkey Hills (East Granby)
West Britain (Bristol)
West Hartford
West Hartland
West Simsbury (Canton)
Wintonbury (Bloomfield)
Worthington (Berlin)

MASSACHUSETTS
Belchertown
Milton
Northampton
Southampton
Southwick
Tyringham

NEW YORK
Black Rock (part of Buffalo)
Canadaway
Milton

OHIO
Austinburg
Morgan (part of Morgan Co)

VERMONT
Cornwall

Appendix G

DEDICATION OF THE SITE OF THE

ORIGINAL MEETINGHOUSE, 1958

On October 5, 1958, a committee of five and approximately thirty-five guests gathered at the end of Reverknolls Road, on the original site of the 1754 Northington meetinghouse. The committee was made up of chairman Clarence B. Curtiss (who carved the lettering on the stone), C. Frederick Woodford, Edward T. Prowe, Charles W. and Austin R. Hunter. Also present were three pastors: Reverend Frederick Bailey (West Avon Congregational Church), Reverend E. Jerome Johansen (Avon Congregational Church) and Reverend Harland G. Lewis (First Church, Farmington). In April, the marker had been set in place on a stone that was part of the church's original foundation. The marker read, "Site of the First Meetinghouse in Avon, 1750–1817."

Reverend Johansen said that "Mr. Curtiss is probably the last living person who could say for sure where the first church stood." Mr. Curtiss, who had lived on Waterville Road since 1921, had learned the exact location from his great uncle Naaman Curtis.

Appendix H

HAWLEY COLLECTION PROVENANCE

The Reverend Rufus Hawley estate was acquired by his son Rufus Forward Hawley at Reverend Hawley's death in 1826. Rufus Forward Hawley may have given the collection to his nephew (and Reverend Rufus's grandson) Edward Eugene Hawley when Edward bought the Avonside house in 1837.

Edward Eugene Hawley, upon his death (1868), probably passed it to his daughter Florence Hawley. Florence Hawley, upon her death (1930), probably passed it to her sister Bertha Hawley. Bertha Hawley, upon her death (1934), probably passed it to her nephew Reginald Birney. Reginald Birney, upon his death (1936), passed it to his widow, Grace Johnson Birney. Grace Johnson Birney gave the collection to Robert and Gladys August upon their purchase of the house in 1951. Robert and Gladys August donated the collection in 2002 to the Marian M. Hunter History Room, Avon Free Public Library, Avon, Connecticut.

HAWLEY GENEALOGY

SHORT CHART OF THE CHILDREN OF REVEREND RUFUS HAWLEY (1741–1826) AND DEBORAH KENT HAWLEY (1739–1798), MARRIED SEPTEMBER 25, 1770

Selected list of Zerah Hawley's descendants limited to key names in the story.

1. Timothy Ruggles (June 29, 1771–July 24, 1828)

2. Rufus Forward (April 27, 1773–December 9, 1847)

3. Jesse Dudley (December 7, 1774–September 26, 1851)

4. George Washington (January 26, 1777–1850/1851)

5. Orestes Kent (September 16, 1778–March 21,1847)

6. Zerah (April 14, 1781–March 6,1856)
   Zerah's son: Edward Eugene Hawley (1811–1868)
       Edward's daughter: Mary Christine Hawley Birney (born 1841)

       Mary's nephew, Reginald Birney (1867–1936) married Grace Johnson (1875–1963)

7. Sophia (November 18, 1782–December 11, 1784)

CHURCH MEMBERSHIP AFTER THE FIRE

M embers of today's Avon Congregational Church and the West Avon Congregational Church, 1818–1819, come from the *Minutes of the Second Ecclesiastical Society of Farmington,* 1818–1824, and from the *Records of the Third Church of Christ in Farmington.* Please note that there was a fair amount of what we might today call church shopping occurring. After the meetinghouse fire of 1817 and the building of the two new churches, attendance and loyalties were sometimes fluid. A person might show up in another church's records in later years.

This list includes those who may have been at church at a moment in time in 1818–19. Women's names for the West Avon Congregational Church have not been located. My thanks to Jeannie Parker for her research on this topic.

THE WEST AVON CONGREGATIONAL CHURCH

Called in 1818 the Second Ecclesiastical Society of Farmington

Samuel Alford, Charles Alling, Richard Bacon, Abner Chidsey, Anson Chidsey, Zaccheus Chidsey, Timothy Darren, Stanley Day, Thomas Day, Erastus Hart, Linus Hart, Obed Hart, Rufus Forward Hawley,

Reuben Horsford, Joshua Kilbourn (chorister), Ebenezer Miller, Romanta Porter, David Sperry, Ashbel Thomson, Cyrus Thomson, Levi Thomson, Thadeus Lot Thomson, Ashbel Tillotson, Chauncey Tillotson, D.N. Tillotson, Hezekiah Tillotson, Oliver Tillotson, Orrin Tillotson, Theodore Wolcott, Asaph Woodford, Coreb Woodford, Roger Woodford, Alanson Woodruff, Francis Woodruff, Gedor Woodruff, Micah Woodruff

THE AVON CONGREGATIONAL CHURCH

Called in 1819 the United Religious Association of Farmington

Lucy Bishop, Samuel Bishop, Thomas F. Bishop, Johnson Booth, Lucy Brockway, Joshua Bulkley, Nathan Case, Thomas Clark, Damaris C. Deming, Dan Deming, Bartholomew Chidsey, Samuel Dickinson, Susannah Dickinson, David Fowler, Rosanna Gillet, Eli Gillit, Isaac Gillet, Lester Gillit, Obadiah Gillet, Silas Goff, Silas Goff Jr., Thankful Goff, David Goodhue, Abner Hart, Elizabeth Hart, Hosea Hart, Joanna Hart, Nathan Lewis, Damaris C. Marshall, Preserved Marshall, Elijah Miller, Martha Miller, Isaiah North, Joseph North, Pantha North, George Norton, Ichabod Norton, Darrin Sperry, Gamahel Sperry, Joel Sperry Jr., Dorcas Talbot, Louisa Thompson, Minerva Thompson, Asa Thomson, Ashbel Thomson, Uriel Thomson, Ashbel Webster Jr., Amos Wheeler, Joel Wheeler, Jeremiah Willcox, Josiah Willcox, Rosanna Willcox, Elijah Woodford, Ester Woodford, Francis Woodford, George B. Woodford, Mary Woodford, Olive Woodford, Orvis Woodford, Romanta Woodford, Sarah Woodford, Selah Woodford, William Woodford, Francis Woodruff. (Illegible: Ebenezer Ha....; Nathan Con...; Silas....; Luther W. Ha....; ....Woodford)

WITHDREW FROM THE SECOND ECCLESIASTICAL SOCIETY OF FARMINGTON (WEST AVON CONGREGATIONAL CHURCH)

November 1818 and January 1819

David H. Gleason, Gideon B. Hart, Lot Hawley, Reuben Hawley Jr., Romanta Hawley, Truman Hawley, William Kilbourn, Chauncey Lusk, James North, David Porter, Sidney Porter, William Porter, Selah Woodford for Austin Thomson as his guardian, Asahek Woodruff, George Wolcott. (Illegible: Samuel....)

NOTES

INTRODUCTION

Reverend Rufus Hawley's seventeen missing journals are for 1770, 1773, 1775, 1776, 1777, 1779, 1781, 1782, 1786, 1788, 1793, 1796, 1801, 1803, 1804, 1805 and 1809. The surviving journals, from 1763 to 1812, are in the collection of the Marian Hunter History Room at the Avon Free Public Library, Avon, Connecticut.

RUFUS HAWLEY, 1741–1762

The date Rufus began school at the academy was possibly October 18, 1762. Justus Forward wrote that Rufus went to Hatfield at that time, returning to Belchertown two months later (December 8, 1762) with his academy friend Augustus Diggins.

Bates, *Records of the Society*, 51.

Forward, Rev. J., Diary, "Godly & Learned" and "Honored Me," May 22, 1767.

Ibid., *Duty of Christ's Ministers*, R. Hawley's "Earnest Desire," "Learned Education" and "Difficulties," 48.

OUR LITTLE COLLEDGE

I am indebted to Dr. Kevin Sweeney, whose dissertation, "River Gods and Related Minor Dieties," contains his research on the academy at Hatfield. The academy opened in late 1762 after eight years of planning by Reverend Stephen Williams, Reverend Solomon Williams and their relatives and friends. These founders lived in a world of "mansion houses, rural gentility, and political power," wrote Dr. Sweeney (vol. 2, 679–680).

Joseph Forward's last words included a reference to his slave, Jenny, as recorded by his son Reverend Justus Forward in the "Dying Charge of Ensign Joseph Forward, 1766." A transcription of the document contains this reference on pages 6–7.

A PLEASANT QUARTER

In Rufus Hawley's Yale class of 1767, seven of the twenty-four students became pastors: Reverend Amos Butler (pastor of Williamsburg, Massachusetts), Reverend Dr. Nathaniel Emmons (Wrentham, Massachusetts), Reverend Rufus Hawley (Northington, Connecticut), Reverend Joseph Lyman (Hatfield, Massachusetts), Jehu Minor (South Britain, Connecticut), Reverend Isaiah Potter (Lebanon, New Haven) and Reverend Samuel Wales (Milford, Connecticut).

Bickford, *Farmington*, 111.

Kelly, *Yale*, "Tomme Clap," 72. The comment by Jonathan Trumbell, "Condemn'd each day," was originally published in 1772 and is cited on p. 82.

THE WORK OF THE MINISTRY

Forward, Rev. J., *Duty of Christ's Ministers*, 42–47.

UNSPEAKABLE GIFTS

Barber, *Barbour Collection*, 443.

Barber's *Suffield*, 133, noted the marriage of "Revd Rufus Hawley and Deborah Kent." Possibly Reverend Ebenezer Gay Jr. of Suffield and Reverend Timothy Pitkin of Farmington both performed the service, as suggested in an e-mail from Reverend Evans Sealand, archivist of the United Church of Christ, Connecticut Conference, September 15, 2008.

Connecticut Courant, Lexell's Comet, July 16, 1770.

Gleason, "Inventory," December 3, 1770.

Farmington Probate Records for 1770, 101–04.

Mackie, *Avon*, "A Man Was Flogged," 23.

West Avon Congregational Church Vital Records. In the twenty years from 1773 to 1792, the Northington parish vital records list fifty-nine marriages. Twenty of the brides delivered their babies two to seven months later. Not one of these babies, perhaps premature, was recorded as stillborn. While being cautious in drawing conclusions, this suggests the possibility that during this twenty-year span, 34 percent of the women were pregnant at the time of their marriages.

TREAT ME AS SHE OUGHT

The wool the women brought to Deborah Hawley at the party on June 8, 1778, was probably about sixty skeins of fiber, representing about half a day's work for each of the women.

Bates, *Records of the Society*, Rev. Booge's December 29, 1776 release of Timothy and Rachel Hawley from church of Turkey Hills to Northington, 18.

Bouton, "A Model for Reflection," 14–19.

Gleason, Day Book, "Don't Remember Text" of a sermon by Reverend Hawley, August 22, 1779.

Mackie, *Avon*, story of Joseph Hart and his son, 23.

Records of the General Association, "Penitent Hearts," 96.

DID BUT LITTLE

Laurel Thatcher Ulrich describes housekeeping in *A Midwife's Tale*, 141. In the late eighteenth century, newly married couples in New England went to housekeeping weeks after a wedding ceremony, when everything was ready for them to do so. During the six weeks or so after a wedding, the bride often stayed at her parents' home until the time was right to depart. This amount of time, which varied, often included neighborly visits among those in the community.

Farmington Probate Records. Timothy Hawley's will, November 9, 1781; proved August 4, 1788.

U.S. Census of Farmington for 1790.

LIFE'S A DREAM

On the Sunday, May 11, when Reverend Rufus Hawley baptized his grandsons Ruggles and Imri, he preached from Psalm 75, verse 4, "all day."

The Marshall Tavern was located at what is today the southwest corner of the intersection of Route 44 and Route 10 at Nod Road, kitty-corner to the Avon Old Farms Inn. In 1932, architect Henry Kelly examined the former Marshall tavern before the State Department of Transportation had it demolished. Kelly found evidence of a circular bar in a room painted pale pink with brown wall stenciling. On the first floor were two parlors, a dining room, many fireplaces and a kitchen ell in the rear. The tavern's second floor was one large ballroom with a vaulted ceiling and a bench around the perimeter. Kelly said, "There is a pleasant, sunny, cheerful atmosphere about this old room that is hard to describe. Is it because of the many windows about the three sides of the room; or is it from some lingering 'human radiation' left by the many gay and happy generations of merry-makers who flocked here from miles around upon so many social occasions?" Terry, *Old Inns of Connecticut*, 54–57. Henry Kelly's 1933 Marshall Tavern report is in the collection of the Avon Free Public Library History Room.

Hawley Land Records, vol. 30, 346–47 (1794); vol. 31, 248 (1795); vol. 31, 94 (1797).

I AWOKE THIS MORNING

Brown, *Genealogical History*.
Connecticut Courant, Deborah Hawley's Death Notice, April 16, 1798, 3.
Hawley E., "Uncommonly Kind and Agreeable," 33–34.
U.S. Treasury Direct Tax. "Minister of Gospel" in 1798 report for Northington.

MY SONS AT NEWCONNECTICUT

Rufus and Elizabeth Hawley's trip to Ohio was June 24 to September 14, 1811. Covering thirty-one miles in a day was common. The journal records the itinerary (some spellings may be incorrect), and stops in chronological order were:

Norfolk, Green River, Greenbush, Albany, Schenectady, Palatine, preached at a schoolhouse in Richfield, Litchfield, Lenox, Clinton, Me[cthus?], preached at an unknown location, Bloomfield, traveled to a place west of the Genesee River, Caladonia, Batavia, Buffalo, preached at Black Rock, to the side of Lake Erie, Cattaraugus, Pomfret, preached at Erie, Elk [or Elkbridge], Ashtabula, to Dr. Hawley's of Austinburgh, to Timothy Hawley's house in Morgan, to Jesse D. Hawley's house, preached at Austinburg, returned to Timothy's at Morgan, went to Jesse D. Hawley's house, returned to Timothy Hawley's in Morgan; preached at Morgan, to Smithfield, Vienna, Howland, Warren and preached in or near there. Met Jesse in Mesopotamia, traveled to Windsor and to Jesse Hawley's. Preached at Morgan, went back to Jesse's, and then Timothy's, and left Morgan. Preached then in Austinburg.

On August 19, 1811, the Hawleys set out for home with Orestes's daughter Cybelia Hawley, age thirty-two:

Saw Timothy again; Rode to Walnut Crick and Chetauquit, and preached at Canadaway and preached again in a home. Rode to Buffalo, Clarvenie?, Batavia, Caladonia, West Bloomfield, Canandaigua, Geneva. Crossed Caygua Lake, and parted with his son Timothy. Preached at Milton, and rode to Homer where they saw Gideon Curtis, Elizabeth's son. Next stop was Duriter; preached at Smithfield, rode to Litchfield, Chatham, Canaan, Spencertown, Sheffield, Green River.

Rufus and Elizabeth Hawley returned home Saturday, September 14, 1811, and he preached the next day.

Barber, *Record and Documentary History*, "Stricken with Palsy" comment by Reverend Samuel Stebbins, 350–51.

Bickford, *Voices of the New Republic*, vol. 2, 46–75.

Connecticut Evangelical Magazine (September 1800), Reverend Rufus Hawley's article, 102–04; account by Reverend Joseph Washburn (May 1801), 422.

Hawley, E., *Hawley Record*, 471.

R. Hawley's letter to John Treadwell, June 12, 1804.

Tarbox, *Diary of Thomas Robbins*, "Mr Hawley…A Minister from Connecticut," vol. 1, October 18, 1805.

WE SPEND OUR YEARS

"For all our days are passed away in thy wrath: we spend our years as a tale that is told." "We spend our years" is from Psalm 90, v. 9. Verse 10 in that psalm would also have spoken directly to Rufus: "The days of our years are threescore and ten; and if by reason of strength they be fourscore years, yet is their strength labour and sorrow; for it is soon cut off, and we fly away."

Silliman, *Remarks Made on a Short Tour*, 30–31, was written when he was a professor at Yale; italics in the text are in the original. Benjamin Silliman's quotation is also in Barber, *Connecticut Historical Collections*, 63, with this additional line by Silliman: "Men were not parading in foreign broadcloth, nor the women flaunting in foreign silks and muslins, but they appeared in domestic fabrics, and both men and women were dressed with simplicity."

Reverend Justus Forward's last entry, on February 25, 1814 (after keeping a diary since 1752), was "This Day 58 years I was ordained to the work of the gospel ministry here [in Belchertown] and have seen great changes, experienced great trials, and also much of the protecting care of God's Providence."

CATCH'D ON FIRE, 1817–1819

Connecticut Courant, comments by Serepta Gillette in an article about her grandson John Andrews, September 9, 1919, 8.

Silliman, *Remarks on a Tour*, 30–31. While Silliman does not call the church by its original name—the Third Church in Farmington—his route is clear. He traveled west on the Albany Turnpike, down Talcott Mountain (also known as Avon Mountain) and past the Avon Congregational Church. The Avon Congregational Church was placed on the National Register of Historic Places in 1972. Martha Hubbell's remarks in *Shady Side*, 238; description of "agricultural people," 240.

West Avon Congregational Church, *Centennial Commemoration*, Reverend Joel Grant's sermon, 11.

Woodruff, diary, March 10–12, 1819. Sometimes the artist stayed overnight.

MR. HAWLEY ENTERTAINED US WELL

"Anxiety" and "Regard for Duty," in Timothy Hawley letter to Zerah Hawley, January 27, 1826.

Betsy Gleason's spoons in Thomas Gleason's letter to Major Elon Gleason, April 9, 1826.

Connecticut Courant, death notice of Reverend Rufus Hawley, January 10, 1826.

Elizabeth Hawley as "kind" and Rufus Forward Hawley as "cold and indifferent" in a letter from Thomas and Elizabeth Gleason to his brothers in Hartford, October 20, 1825.

Farmington Probate Records, Reverend Rufus Hawley's will, 1820.

Gleason, letter, July 1821.

Hawley, E., "Heraldic, Historic and Genealogic Exposition," Rufus Hawley's half-century sermon of December 1819.

Hawley, Z. *Journal of a Tour*, "Unwilling to Live," 3.

Religious Intelligencer, death notice of Rev. Rufus Hawley's death, January 26, 1826, 541.

"Such manners" and "Never Received a Cent" in Rufus F. Hawley's letter to Zerah Hawley, July 21, 1826.

"Sweep the Whole" in Timothy Hawley's letter to Zerah Hawley, July 14, 1826.

Tarbox, *Diary of Thomas Robbins*, "Small Meeting," vol. I, 919; "Quite Feeble," "Increase and Prospered," 955.

A CONFUSED HEAP OF RECORDS

On May 5, 1830, the Connecticut General Assembly approved the incorporation of the town of Avon.

Hawley, E., "Heraldic, Historic and Genealogic Exposition"; "Engaged in Agriculture" in his description of Zerah Hawley.

West Avon Congregational Church, *Centennial Commemoration*, Reverend Steven Hubbell's "representative of the old family," "sad was the sight" and "chasm to history," 37–38, November 20, 1851.

YOU HAVE TO GO

"Silly company" is the handwritten description of a group photo from a caption in the Birney photograph album, probably written by Reginald or Grace Birney.

CLOSELY ON THE LINE OF MIRACLES

Bartlett, *Memorial History of Hartford County*, "Not a Man of Brilliant Parts," vol. 2, 11.

Hawley, E., *Hawley Record*, "Closely on a Line of Miracles, v.

Hurlburt, *Farmington Town Clerks*, "Able and Worthy," 340.

Tarbox, *Diary of Thomas Robbins*, vol. 1, "Venerable," 80n; pamphlets cost $1.88 in July 19, 1826, vol. 1, 20.

West Avon Congregational Church, *Centennial Commemoration*, "A Man Full of Faith" from Steven Hubbell's address, 39.

APPENDIX B

The Hart farmhouse is at 72 Cider Brook Road.

Bickford, *Farmington*, 200.

MacKie, *Avon*, 8, 16.

APPENDIX C

Contributions to the Ecclesiastical History of Connecticut, "Ripe for a Society," vol. 1, 344.

MacKie, *Avon*, events of 1750, 74.

West Avon Congregational Church, *Centennial Commemoration*, Reverend Booge made his "half-member" comment during a visit to the West Simsbury Church on December 22, 1754, 35; "Reason to Hope" in Grant's *Centennial Sermon*, 11–16.

APPENDIX F

Elias Hawley, *Hawley Record*, 471.

SELECTED BIBLIOGRAPHY

August, Robert. *Avonside.* Reminiscences by Robert August. Hawley-August Collection, Marion Hunter History Room, Avon Free Public Library, Avon, CT.

Avon Land Records. Town Clerk's Office, Avon, CT.

Avon Probate Records. Town Clerk's Office, Avon, CT.

Barbour, John Warner. *Connecticut Historical Collections.* New Haven, CT: Durrie & Peck, 1836.

Bartlett, Matthew H. In *The Memorial History of Hartford County, 1633–1884.* Edited by J. Hammond Trumbull. 2 vols. Boston: Edward L. Osgood, 1886.

Bates, Albert C., ed. *Records of the Society or Parish of Turkey Hills now the Town of East Granby, Connecticut, 1737–1901.* Hartford, CT: Albert Carlos Bates, 1901.

———. *Vital Records of East Granby, Connecticut, 1737–1886.* Hartford, CT: Albert Carlos Bates, 1947.

Bickford, Christopher P. *Farmington in Connecticut.* Canaan, NH: Phoenix Publishing for the Farmington Historical Society, 1982.

———, ed. *Voices of the New Republic, Connecticut Towns 1800-1832.* Vols. 1 and 2. New Haven: Connecticut Academy of Arts and Sciences, 2003.

Birney Family Photograph Album. Hawley-August Collection, Marian Hunter History Room, Avon Free Public Library, Avon, CT.

Brown, Abiel. *Genealogical History of the Early Settlers of West Simsbury, now Canton, Conn.* Hartford, CT: Case, Tiffany and Company, 1856.

Clap, Thomas. *The Annals or History of Yale College, 1700–1766*. N.p.: John Hotchkiss, 1766.

Connecticut Courant, April 10, 1798; April 16, 1798; January 10, 1826.

Connecticut Courant and Weekly Intelligencer

Connecticut Evangelical Magazine, 1800–1814. Archives of the Connecticut Conference of the United Church of Christ, Hartford, CT.

Contributions to the Ecclesiastical History of Connecticut. 2 vols. New Haven, CT: William L. Kinglsey, 1861. Reprint, Hartford, CT: Bond Press for the Connecticut Conference of the United Church of Christ, 1973.

Dexter, Franklin Bowditch. *Biographical Sketches of the Graduates of Yale College*. Vol. 2, May 1745–May 1763. New York: Henry Holt and Company, 1896.

———. *Biographical Sketches of the Graduates of Yale College*. Vol. 3, May 1763–July 1778. New York: Henry Holt and Company, 1903.

Doolittle, Mark. *Historical Sketch of the Congregational Church in Belchertown, Massachusetts*. Northampton, MA: Hopkins, Bridgeman & Co., 1852. Collection of the Connecticut Historical Society, Hartford, CT.

Edwards, Jonathan, Jr. *Salvation of All Men Strictly Examined*. New Haven, CT: A. Morse, 1790.

Farmington Land Records. Town Clerk's Office, Farmington Town Hall, Farmington, CT.

Farmington Probate Records. Town Clerk's Office, Farmington Town Hall, Farmington, CT.

———. Inventory of Rev. Rufus Hawley, March 8, 1826. Town Clerk's Office, Farmington Town Hall, Farmington, CT.

Farmington Town Records. Town Clerk's Office, Farmington Town Hall, Farmington, CT.

Forward, Joseph. "Dying Charge of Ensign Joseph Forward, May 22, 1766." Collection of the Stone House Museum of the Belchertown Historical Association, Belchertown, MA.

Forward, Reverend Justus. Diary, 1767. Hyde Collection, MS AM 564. Houghton Library, Harvard University.

———. Diaries, 1762, 1766, 1785, 1786, 1797. Octavo Volume "F." Courtesy American Antiquarian Society, Worcester, MA.

———. Diaries, 1778, 1812. Justus Forward Papers, MS 219, Manuscript and Archives, Yale University Library. [The other diaries at Yale are for 1759, 1794, 1795, 1796, 1802, 1805 and 1814. The journal for 1759 is marked "No. 8," indicating that his first journal would have been from 1752.]

———. *The Duty of Christ's Ministers, to hold faith and a good conscience, and the way to perform it, illustrated in a Sermon, preached at the ordination of the Reverend*

Mr. Rufus Hawley. Hartford, CT: Printed by Ebenezer Watson, 1771. Collection of the Connecticut Historical Society, Hartford, CT. [Forty-page sermon; original copy handwritten by Reverend Justus Forward, in Justus Forward Papers, Sermons 1769, MS 219, Manuscript and Archives, Yale University Library.]

———. "Forensic Disputes or Questions." Handwritten booklet while a student at Yale, 1752. Justus Forward Papers, MS 219, Manuscripts and Archives, Yale University Library.

Gleason, David. Day Book, 1779, 1785, 1794. Folder 5, Sheet 2(1). Gleason Papers. Collection of the Farmington Room, Farmington Library, Farmington, CT.

Gleason, Thomas. Letter to Major Elon Gleason, April 9, 1826. Gleason Papers, Folder 5, Sleeve 2(2). Farmington Room, Farmington Library, Farmington, CT.

Hawley-August Collection. Marian Hunter History Room, Avon Free Public Library, Avon, CT. [Includes photographs, maps, genealogies, family papers of the Hawley family and letters, including those of Rufus Hawley's sons, grandson Edward Eugene Hawley and great-grandson and Civil War veteran Edward Hawley, 1763–twentieth century. Donated by Robert and Gladys August.]

Hawley, Edward Eugene. "Heraldic, Historic and Genealogic Exposition of Hawley." Booklet 2-138. Hawley-August Collection, Marian Hunter History Room, Avon Free Public Library, Avon, CT.

Hawley, Elias S. *Hawley Record.* Buffalo, NY: E.H. Hutchinson & Co., 1890. Collection of the Connecticut Historical Society, Hartford, CT.

Hawley, Reverend Rufus. *Connecticut Evangelical Magazine* (September 1800): 102–04.

———. Estate Inventory, March 8, 1826. Collection of the Connecticut State Library, Hartford, CT. [A copy is in the Hawley-August Collection, Marian Hunter History Room, Avon Free Public Library, Avon, CT.]

———. Journals, 1763–1812. Marian Hunter History Room, Avon Free Public Library, Avon, CT.

———. Letter to John Treadwell, June 12, 1804. Treadwell Papers, Connecticut State Library, Record Group 69.25. [A copy is in the Marian Hunter History Room, Avon Free Public Library.]

Hawley, Timothy. Letter, November 18, 1808, from Timothy Hawley in Morgan, Ohio, to Reverend Justus Forward in Belchertown, MA. Justus Forward Papers, MS 219, Yale University Library.

Hawley, Zerah. *A Journal of a Tour Through Connecticut, Massachusetts, New-York, the Northern Part of Pennsylvania and Ohio, Including a Years Residence in that Part of the State of Ohio, Styled New Connecticut or Western Reserve. In which is Given a Description of the Country, Climate, Soil, Products, Animals, Buildings, Manners of the People, State of Society, Population, &c. From Actual and Careful Observation.* New Haven, CT: S. Converse, 1822.

Hubbell, Martha S. *The Shady Side; or, Life in a Country Parsonage.* Boston: John P. Jewett and Company, 1853.

Hurlburt, Mabel S. *Farmington Town Clerks and Their Times, 1645–1940.* Hartford, CT: Press of Finlay Brothers, 1943. [Contains a 1829 map of Northington.]

Kelley, Brooks Mather. *Yale.* New Haven, CT: Yale University Press, 1974.

Kelly, Henry. "Report on the Marshall Tavern, 1933." Collection of the Marian Hunter History Room, Avon Free Public Library, Avon, CT.

MacKie, Mary-Frances. *Avon, Connecticut.* Canaan, NH: Phoenix Publishing for the Avon Historical Society, 1988.

McGuinness, William, Jr. "Avon Men in the Mexican War, Civil War, and Spanish-American War." Avon, Connecticut, November 21, 1987. Paper in the collection of the Marian Hunter History Room, Avon Free Public Library, Avon, CT.

Moulton, Reverend J.W. *Historical Address, delivered at the Centennial Celebration, September 7 and 8, 1919, of the Avon Congregational Church.* Collection of the Avon Congregational Church, Avon, CT.

Porter, Noah, Jr. *A Historical Discourse.* Hartford, CT: L. Skinner, 1841.

Records of the General Association of ye Colony of Connecticut, 1738–1799. Hartford, CT: Press of the Case, Lockwood & Brainard Company, 1888.

Romer, Robert H. *Slavery in the Connecticut Valley of Massachusetts.* Florence, MA: Levellers Press, 2009.

Schoelwer, Susan P. *Connecticut Needlework: Women, Art, and Family, 1740–1840.* Hartford, CT: Connecticut Historical Society, 2010.

Silliman, Benjamin. *Remarks Made on a Short Tour Between Hartford and Quebec in the Autumn of 1819.* 2nd ed. New Haven, CT: S. Converse, 1824.

Silverman, Kenneth. *The Life and Times of Cotton Mather.* New York: Harper & Row, 1984.

Skeel, Emily, ed. *Notes on the Life of Noah Webster.* Vol. 2. Privately printed, 1912.

Springman, Mary Jane, and Betty Finnell Guinan. *East Granby, the Evolution of a Connecticut Town.* Canaan, NH: Phoenix Publishing for the East Granby Historical Committee, 1983.

Stanley-Whitman House. "Black Slavery in the 18th Century." Farmington, CT.

Stout, Harry S. *New England Soul: Preaching and Religious Culture in Colonial New England.* New York: Oxford University Press, 1986.

Sweeney, Kevin M. "River Gods and Related Minor Dieties: The Williams Family and the Connecticut River Valley, 1637–1790." 2 vols. PhD. diss., Yale University, 1986.

Tarbox, Increase N., ed. *Diary of Thomas Robbins, D.D., 1796–1854.* 2 vols. Boston: Beacon Press, 1886.

Thompson, Marian E., and Ruth A. Thompson. *Cider Brook Cemetery.* 2 vols. Privately printed, n.d. Collection of the Marian Hunter History Room, Avon Free Public Library, Avon, CT.

———. *The East Avon Cemetery.* 2 vols. Privately printed, 1996. Collection of the Marian Hunter History Room, Avon Free Public Library, Avon, CT.

———. *The West Avon Cemetery.* 2 vols. Privately printed, 1987. Collection of the Marian Hunter History Room, Avon Free Public Library, Avon, CT.

U.S. Census Records for Avon and Farmington, CT.

West Avon Congregational Church (First Church in West Avon, CT). *Centennial Commemoration of the Organization of the First Church in West Avon, Conn., November 20, 1851, Embracing a Sermon by Rev. Joel Grant, pastor of the church;* [and] *an Address by Rev. Stephen Hubbell, pastor of the 2nd* [Avon Congregational] *Church.* Hartford, CT: George D. Jewett, 1851.

———. Minutes, 1753–1835. Transcribed by Ruth Thompson. Collection of the West Avon Congregational Church, Avon, CT.

———. Vital Records, 1752–1861. Collection of the West Avon Congregational Church, Avon, CT. [Hand-copied from the original in the Connecticut State Library. Vital Records database by Nora Howard, 2006. Collection of the Marian Hunter History Room, Avon Free Public Library, Avon, CT.]

White, Lorraine Cook, ed. *The Barbour Collection of Connecticut Town Vital Records: Farmington 1645–1850.* Vol. 12. Baltimore, MD: Genealogical Publishing Co., 1998.

Williams, Mark. *A Tempest in a Small Town: The Myth and Reality of Country Life, Granby, Connecticut, 1680–1940.* Granby, CT: Salmon Brook Historical Society, 1966.

INDEX

Woodford, Daniel 50, 51
Woodford, Dudley 108
Woodford, Elijah 73, 108
Woodford, Esther 82
Woodford, Fanny 82
Woodford, Francis 147
Woodford, Hannah 57
Woodford, Joseph 58
Woodford, Mary 65, 93
Woodford, Mrs. Israel 65
Woodford, Roger 144
Woodford, Samuel 108
Woodford, Selah 108
Woodford, William 39, 79, 93
Woodruff, Aaron 91
Woodruff, Alanson 143, 145
Woodruff, Anne 56
Woodruff, Apheck 115, 118, 120
Woodruff, Buelah 120
Woodruff, Eldad, Jr. 116
Woodruff, Electa 116
Woodruff, Elna 116
Woodruff, Josiah 73
Woodruff, Medad 56
Woodruff, Ozem 115
Woodruff, Romanta 135
Woodruff, Samuel 16
Woodruff, Wilford 14, 118, 120
Woodruff, Zebulon, Jr. 63
Woolen Manufactory 86, 144

Y

Yale 10, 13, 16, 17, 29, 39
yellow fever 117

ABOUT THE AUTHOR

Nora Howard is town historian of Avon, Connecticut, and historian
of the Avon Congregational Church. She is the author of *Stories of
Wethersfield* and the photograph history *Avon*. Mrs. Howard was director of
the historical societies of Avon and
Wethersfield, Connecticut, worked at
the Smithsonian Institution's National
Museum of American History and
served as historian of First Church
of Christ in Wethersfield. Her articles
on local history have appeared in
Wethersfield Life and *Avon Life*, and her
writings have won awards from the
American Association for State and
Local History and the Connecticut
League of Historical Societies. Ms.
Howard earned degrees in American
studies from Hampshire College (BA)
and George Washington University
(MA). As a graduate assistant at the
University of Maryland, she helped
annotate the Samuel Gompers Papers.

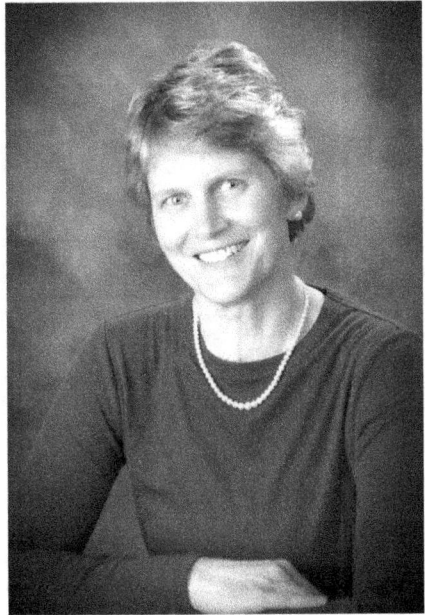

Visit us at
www.historypress.net

www.ingramcontent.com/pod-product-compliance
Lightning Source LLC
Chambersburg PA
CBHW070927150426
42812CB00049B/1558